NEW DIRECTIONS FOR ADULT A

Susan Imel, *Ohio State University*
Ralph G. Brockett, *University of Tennessee, Knoxville*
EDITORS-IN-CHIEF

Creating Practical Knowledge Through Action Research: Posing Problems, Solving Problems, and Improving Daily Practice

B. Allan Quigley
Pennsylvania State University

Gary W. Kuhne
Pennsylvania State University

EDITORS

Number 73, Spring 1997

JOSSEY-BASS PUBLISHERS
San Francisco

CREATING PRACTICAL KNOWLEDGE THROUGH ACTION RESEARCH: POSING
PROBLEMS, SOLVING PROBLEMS, AND IMPROVING DAILY PRACTICE
B. Allan Quigley, Gary W. Kuhne (eds.)
New Directions for Adult and Continuing Education, no. 73
Susan Imel, Ralph G. Brockett, Editors-in-Chief

ISSN 1052–2891   ISBN 0-7879-9816-8

NEW DIRECTIONS FOR ADULT AND CONTINUING EDUCATION is part of The
Jossey-Bass Higher and Adult Education Series and is published quarterly
by Jossey-Bass Inc., Publishers, 350 Sansome Street, San Francisco,
California 94104-1342. Periodicals postage paid at San Francisco, California, and at additional mailing offices. POSTMASTER: Send address
changes to New Directions for Adult and Continuing Education, Jossey-
Bass Inc., Publishers, 350 Sansome Street, San Francisco, California
94104-1342.   •

SUBSCRIPTIONS cost $54.00 for individuals and $90.00 for institutions,
agencies, and libraries.

EDITORIAL CORRESPONDENCE should be sent to the Editor-in-Chief,
Susan Imel, ERIC/ACVE, 1900 Kenny Road, Columbus, Ohio 43210-1090.
E-mail: imel.1@osu.edu.

Cover photograph by Wernher Krutein/PHOTOVAULT © 1990.

Printed in the United States of America on acid-free recycled paper con-
taining 100 percent recovered waste paper, of which at least 20 percent is postconsumer waste.

CONTENTS

EDITORS' NOTES

If you are a teacher, tutor, counselor, or administrator working in adult education and are seeking better ways to address educational problems, this sourcebook may be for you. If you are a researcher, if you are concerned with the future of research in this field, or if you are a policymaker interested in trends in research and practice, this sourcebook should be of interest.

This sourcebook is written on three levels. First, it is intended for educators and trainers of adults in formal settings. The types of formal settings we have in mind include higher education, continuing professional education, corporate training, adult basic and literacy education, and religious education or health education. It is also intended for those working in many of the informal adult education activities, including volunteer training, some types of distance education, and community development work. In any of these settings, action research provides a systematic discovery process that has helped hundreds of adult education practitioners understand, analyze, interpret, and resolve day-to-day problems in the educational workplace.

However, as the saying goes, "Don't get mad, get data." Beyond problem posing and problem solving, a successfully documented action research project can be tried across an entire institution, region, or state (Clift, Veal, Johnson, and Holland, 1990; The Holmes Group, 1990). The extrapolated outcomes of multiple successful projects can be used to make a case for more resources or, at the policy level, to advise and encourage others to attempt the same or similar projects for the improvement of practice across entire regions (McTaggart, 1991).

Second, as a *process* of inquiry, action research encourages one to adopt an enhanced critical perspective on aspects of one's work and work environment (O'Neil and Marsick, 1994). This perspective can make relational and organizational questions "askable" and otherwise sensitive issues "discussable" with new constructive objectivity. We can often begin to act, rather than react, with this new perspective.

Finally, beyond practice, action research offers a distinct challenge to the traditional methodologies and ideologies within adult education (Brooks and Watkins, 1994). At this third level, the assumptions and ideology that underlie action research have brought changes to the ways research has been conducted in the public school system over the past three decades. In fact, collaborating to gain knowledge and sharing the outcomes among all participants has been a research approach used in nontraditional adult education settings for most of this century. Yet, as discussed in Chapter One, our various forms of collaborative research have had less impact on mainstream adult education research than that seen in the K–12 system. The politics and issues that will affect the further growth of action research within the mainstream of adult education in the future are discussed in Chapter One.

How to Read This Sourcebook

Given the different levels and the wide audience this sourcebook is aimed at, it can be read from various starting points. If you are a practitioner wanting to get started on defining and working on a problem, you should begin with Chapter Two, because it gives the nuts and bolts of how to conduct action research. However, to first see how others have used action research, you may want to begin with Chapter Three. Here are case studies purposely chosen to represent a wide range of problems and settings. Chapter Three may also be helpful if you are interested in leading a discussion on action research, if you are teaching this research method, or if you are including action research in a course on research methods.

However, if you are interested in the background of action research in both the adult education and the public school systems, or if you are concerned about some of the critical research issues surrounding the production and legitimation of knowledge in the adult education field, you should begin with Chapter One. This chapter looks at some of the challenges we face in adult education research and practice.

Regardless of where you start, Chapters Four and Five seek to open discussion on the entire topic of action research and the relationship of research to practice. Without active dialogue on the issues that surround research-based knowledge, it will be impossible to bring about the kind of changes that the authors of this volume hope to see in the future.

B. Allan Quigley
Gary W. Kuhne
Editors

References

Brooks, A., and Watkins, K. E. "A New Era for Action Technologies: A Look at the Issues." In A. Brooks and K. E. Watkins (eds.), *The Emerging Power of Action Inquiry Technologies*. New Directions for Adult and Continuing Education, no. 63. San Francisco: Jossey-Bass, 1994.

Clift, R., Veal, M. L., Johnson, M., and Holland, P. "Restructuring Teacher Education Through Collaborative Action Research." *Journal of Teacher Education*, 1990, 41 (2), 52–62.

Holmes Group, The. *Tomorrow's Schools: Principles for the Design of Professional Development Schools*. East Lansing, Mich.: The Holmes Group, 1990.

McTaggart, R. "Principles for Participatory Action Research." *Adult Education Quarterly*, 1991, 3 (41), 168–187.

O'Neil, J., and Marsick, V. "Becoming Critically Reflective Through Action Reflection Learning." In A. Brooks and K. E. Watkins (eds.), *The Emerging Power of Action Inquiry Technologies*. New Directions for Adult and Continuing Education, no. 63. San Francisco: Jossey-Bass, 1994.

B. ALLAN QUIGLEY is associate professor and regional director of adult education at Pennsylvania State University and director of the Pennsylvania Action Research Network.

GARY W. KUHNE is assistant professor of adult education at Pennsylvania State University and an evaluator/trainer in the Pennsylvania Action Research Network.

This chapter discusses issues surrounding the production of research knowledge, including who has the authority to conduct it. The background of action research in the public school system is contrasted with that in the adult education system, and a new framework for research that includes the various forms of collaborative research is presented.

The Role of Research in the Practice of Adult Education

B. Allan Quigley

One of the great ironies of traditional education is that teaching and learning are so inherently concerned with knowledge but those engaged in the education process have so little ownership over the "knowledge products" on which they build their careers. Like a vast corporate enterprise in an Ayn Rand novel, the majority of teachers, counselors, and administrators spend their careers at the receiving end of "manufactured" research products produced in remote university "factories" by unseen research experts. Seen this way, the conventional role of the teaching system is merely to buy and use the products of others.

Whether this depiction is an exaggeration or not, certainly a vast enterprise surrounds the production, marketing, preparation, and evaluation of research-based knowledge in the education field. Whatever the vehicle—textbooks, videos, interactive media, or on-line dissemination—it is not an exaggeration to say that the production of research-based content in authoritative texts is typically considered the domain of the expert researcher. Therefore, ironically, it is the unseen researcher whom few know and few communicate with who "knows what's best for everyone" in the field.

Who Should Produce Knowledge?

The irony of this situation is not that so many educators often have only the vaguest of idea of where the knowledge in their textbooks comes from, or why certain knowledge products come "on the market" while other areas of educational concern seem to languish for decades. The irony, seen from the

I am indebted to Dr. David Deshler for his helpful comments and input to this chapter.

knowledge-product viewpoint, is that so many educators who work hard to develop student independence and learner critical thinking are themselves so dependent, so passive, and ostensibly so uncritical of the entire research process.

For adult educators, the irony is even more poignant. Most of the adult education teachers, tutors, and administrators whom I know work extremely hard to create an interactive, open atmosphere in their classrooms (Knowles, 1980), yet the very opposite exists when it comes to the production of knowledge being used in their classrooms.

It is only in the past two decades that a fledgling public school teacher–based movement has begun to gain momentum in both teaching practice and the literature (Catelli, 1995; Torbert, 1981). This public school movement has grown since the 1970s to the point where Diane Kyle and Ric Hovda (1987) comment on the appeal of action research in today's U.S. schools: "Why has action research captured such interest in the educational community? Why its appeal? What is the hope? Perhaps the most compelling explanation resides in the recognition that educational change has been critically needed, that we have needed new visions of what schools are, of how students learn, and of what constitutes the profession of teaching" (p. 174).

While some in public education have argued that these K–12 teacher efforts are inadequate or unoriginal (for example, van Manen, 1990), the same level of practitioner challenge cannot be found in mainstream adult education— at least not yet. It is true that there are multiple examples of action research being used by teachers and tutors of adults. In adult literacy, for example, action research has been used by teachers and tutors on a statewide basis in Virginia for several years (Cockley, 1993), and in Pennsylvania (Quigley, 1995) it is entering its third year as a statewide initiative. Action research has been advocated for many years on an institutional basis at Teachers College, Columbia University, in New York for literacy work; at Cornell University (for example, Shafer, 1995); at a number of institutions across California (McDonald, 1994); at North Carolina's Literacy South organization for literacy (Pates, 1992); and, depending on the definition used for action research, it has a lengthy history at the Highlander Research and Education Center in New Market, Tennessee, and has been a major presence at the Center for Literacy Studies at the University of Tennessee, Knoxville.

Action research has been used extensively in training and development in corporate America since the late 1940s, when Kurt Lewin founded it in this country (Lewin, 1948; Weisbord, 1987). Outside of the United States, action research has been used extensively in adult education environmental, agricultural, and health settings (Whyte, 1991). It is has been used in the development of businesses and business cooperatives in thousands of international projects (Deshler and Hagan, 1989; Shafer, 1995).

However, all of this activity through more than half a century has not brought a direct challenge to the mainstream of adult education research. Why not? In part, it is because most of this activity has occurred outside of the mainstream. Unlike the K–12 system, the production of knowledge in adult education arises out of a very complex range of practice settings. And, in part, it is because the traditional mainstream of adult education is remarkably slow in being affected by change. As will be seen, one can argue that the formal mainstream even resists change from the nontraditional areas of its own field.

Who Owns Knowledge Through Research?

The issue of who owns and controls research, as David Deshler and Nancy Hagan expressed it in the *Handbook of Adult and Continuing Education* (1989, p. 153), has been attracting more and more attention in the adult education literature in recent years. The assumptions of what constitutes legitimate research are also being questioned. I will argue in this chapter that despite our history of slow change, the nature of these questions and the growth of the action research movement among mainstream practitioners will soon constitute one of the greatest challenges traditional adult education research will face as it enters the next millennium.

Growing Awareness at the Academic Level

The question of ownership of knowledge was raised as recently as the 1996 Commission of Professors annual meeting, where two of three researchers speaking on a panel concerning research trends in adult education chose to focus on the growing interest of adult education practitioners in action research; to these two, this was a trend waiting to be embraced. The third panelist spoke to the growing challenges to traditional research in general. In the literature, adult education's corpus of research and research methods have been repeatedly classified, categorized, and criticized (for example, Deshler and Hagan, 1989; Jensen, Liveright, and Hallenbeck, 1964; Merriam and Simpson, 1984; Rubenson, 1989). However, it is becoming widely accepted that the underlying research issue for the field is not codification of methods. The deeper issue behind the repeated classifications of research—the competing classifications, one might say—is the conflict among ideological understandings of what the practice of adult education "should be for" (Cervero, 1991). And, in my view, what types of research and research methods should be acceptable to support the competing purposes of this field constitutes the growing academic debate.

Many academics have been saying for years, as Kyle and Hovda argued in the public system, that the mainstream of adult education needs alternative visions of what our traditional adult education settings are, how students learn, and what constitutes the profession of adult teaching (see Cunningham, 1989; Cervero, 1991; Peters, 1991). One of the most promising changes in recent years is the growing awareness of the rights of participants in research. This newfound awareness opens the door to one of the central tenets of action research, namely, that there is an obligation to the "researched" as well as to the method of research (Hall, 1979; McTaggart, 1991; Quigley, Dean, and Lawson, 1994; Tom and Sork, 1994). Merriam, for instance, has cautioned the field that "adult education is indeed a moral activity in which we intervene in the lives of women and men in, we hope, positive ways. Research, then, should be conducted with this in mind. . . . We should care what happens with and to our participants. The question of whether competing research paradigms will or should coexist fades in importance when set against this larger moral imperative of our practice" (1991, pp. 59–60). Whether this sort of moral sensitivity is actually a case of adult education core ethical values inexorably rising to the surface (Cunningham, 1989), or the impact of long-standing nontraditionalists' arguments (Deshler and Hagan, 1989), or simply part of the widespread challenge to old absolutes in our postmodern era (Boshier, 1994; Briton, 1996), there is certainly a growing realization that "programs of graduate study should present research as a value-laden, moral activity" (Merriam, 1991, p. 60). As obvious as this statement may seem, a view such as this from within the mainstream would have been highly controversial in the 1950s, 1960s, 1970s, and even the early 1980s (Wilson, 1992) in adult education.

The promising sign, therefore, is that research in the mainstream has begun to be demystified. As Merriam states, program planning, teaching, and counseling are "moral activities" (1991, p. 61). Likewise, "research should also be seen as an integral part of our practice" (Merriam, 1991, p. 61), with moral implications. The overwhelming question, "who produces, controls, and benefits from research?" (Deshler, 1991, p. 413), is becoming a central concern in discussions of research (for example, Blunt, 1994). It is in the context of this growing question that action research can play an important role in the coming years. Possibly, action research, with its collaborative approach and mainstream application, is a methodology whose time has finally come in our field.

Effects of the "Ideological Divide" in Adult Education

As noted earlier, the history and structures of adult education are not the same as the public schools' in the United States (Grattan, 1955; Stubblefield and Keane, 1994). One of the most significant differences between these two histories arises from the delivery structures of the two systems. Adult education has not grown out of an institutional history as has the public system. Notwithstanding the many definitions of what activities are included in adult education, most will agree with Courtney (1989) that "adult education might be seen to embrace a variety of prominent, visible, social activities lying somewhere between schooling and recreation" (p. 15). Ours is an extremely diverse field.

Besides formal adult education—"schooling," as Courtney refers to it—where curricula and credit evaluation systems are formally organized by institutions, adult education has a history of informal learning beginning at least with Benjamin Franklin's famous Junto discussion groups in Colonial America (Grattan, 1955). Our history of informal learning extends through the volatile immigrant workers' halls at the turn of the century (Schied, 1993) to community work in the hills of Tennessee (Adams, 1975) and the urban ghettoes of cosmopolitan cities (Alinsky, 1972; Cunningham, 1989). These types of activities, together with the plethora of general interest classes sponsored by social organizations and educational institutions today, are examples of informal adult education in this country.

Adult education also flourishes in a third, nonformal venue. Here is a world of adult education that Coombs has referred to as the "truly lifelong learning process" (quoted in Lowe, 1975, p. 24). Here, typically, is self-directed learning, which goes on with no outside instruction at all (Tough, 1971). Nonformal is where "adults inform themselves about life and its possibilities" (Courtney, 1989, p. 18) in a natural, even "accidental" manner, as Coolie Verner used to express it (Verner and Booth, 1964).

With adult education's variety in at least three venues and its broad range of accessibility to learning, one might think that it also has a history of learner ownership of knowledge and knowledge production. In the nonformal and informal traditions, it indeed does have such a history, and we need more recognition and documentation of this, as I will discuss (Cunningham, 1989). In formal settings, adult education's history is much the same as K–12's with respect to knowledge production. It is the ideological division between the formal, or so-called traditional, and the nonformal/informal, or "nontraditional" arenas that is significant for this discussion.

In the United States, adult education has a century-old history of ideological conflict over its goals and purposes. To oversimplify, formal adult education has developed based on traditional school assumptions, for reasons historians such as Amy Rose (1989) have discussed. Rose has shown how the professional organization of adult educators—the American Association for Adult Education—was in fact the beginning of educator exclusivity through the attempt to professionalize adult education at that time (see also Stubblefield and Keane, 1994).

The AAAE began in 1926 with a distinct focus on liberal adult education (Stubblefield and Keane, 1994). Consciously or not, the early philosophical decision was to include conventional educators with a liberal education background and exclude people such as worker educators, community educators, and adult educators concerned with social justice (Stubblefield and Keane, 1994). The AAAE and the beginning of professionalization was a defining moment in more ways than one.

As Stubblefield and Keane (1994) explain, "In its early years, the AAAE appeared to be impartial by refusing to associate with any social causes or special groups" (p. 194). Our founders "held that adult education in a democracy must create informed citizens, promote tolerance and understanding of differences, and maintain social stability" (Stubblefield and Keane, 1994). Subsequently, as Wilson (1992) has shown, this classic liberal-schooling philosophy pointed adult education toward university researchers in the 1930s in order develop a "professional" research base. In this way, empirical positivism and traditional scientific rationalism became mainstream adult education's answer to the question of what constitutes research for almost four decades (Wilson, 1992).

The other excluded "nontraditional" forms of practice were reluctantly recognized as exactly that—nontraditional practice—in the expanding adult education mainstream. Over time, the attendant research methods of the untraditional have gone unrecognized. Here, then, is the ideological divide that must be considered when discussing how adult education has arrived at knowledge deemed "legitimate."

Three decades after the formation of the AAAE and just as the field was trying to build itself into a respected discipline in academe with the publication of *Adult Education: Outlines of an Emerging Field of University Study* (Jensen, Liveright, and Hallenbeck, 1964; commonly called the Black Book), Webster Cotton described how adult education had grown out of "two great traditions." As Cotton explained at the time, adult education has grown out of a "social reformist tradition" and a "professional tradition" (1964, p. 84). As he saw it, the long-established social reformist tradition of the field was inspired by "idealism, moral enthusiasm and intellectual vigor" (p. 84). The social reformist tradition sprang from Britain's *1919 Report* and the work of early British adult educators such as R. H. Tawney, Albert Mansbridge, and Basil Yeaxlee. However, this was exactly the sort of "naively idealistic" group not invited to the formation of the AAAE. By the 1960s and Jensen, Liveright, and Hallenbeck's Black Book, here was the type of adult educator that university-based adult educators were trying to separate themselves from. As Cotton put it, the "professional tradition" arose, "at least partially, in reaction against the social reformist orientation" (1964, p. 84). The professional standards for the field were effectively "repudiating the *utopianism* of the social reformist tradition" (p. 118). And, I have argued elsewhere (Quigley, 1991) that this ideological division has continued in adult education up to the present.

Not surprisingly, the history of the social reform tradition is not well documented in the adult education literature (Cunningham, 1989). However, to assume that the social reformist educational programs were universally rudderless and without research systems would be a mistake. Both in the United States and Canada, adult educators working outside the self-declared mainstream have used multiple forms of qualitative—or naturalistic (Guba and Lincoln, 1981; Garrison and Shale, 1994)—research methodologies. A few of these adult educators have documented their inquiries as part of Freirean approaches to social action, such as Saint Mary's Community Education Center in Chicago (Heaney, 1977) and its sister school, Instituto del Progresso Latino, run by Latino learners for Latino learners (Cunningham, 1989).

Perhaps the most famous example is the Highlander Research and Education Center in New Market, Tennessee. It has an extensive library that has been used for more than a half century by groups who come to investigate, reflect on, and form strategies to address the issues they face (Gaventa and Horton, 1981). A famous community-based project in Canada was the Antigonish Movement in Nova Scotia, where the region's fishing industry and local economy were saved through the St. Francis Xavier University Extension Division with collaborative learning and inquiry processes of adult education (Cookson, 1989; Conger, 1974). Through the Coady Institute at St. Francis Xavier University, the same principles of collaborative research at the community level are still systematically taught and fostered in developing countries around the world.

Despite appearances of adult education action research in the public school literature, including examples from Xerox Corporation (Pace and Argona, 1991) and the labor movement (Costanza, 1991; Whyte, 1991), still to be documented in the adult education literature are the actual research methods of collaborative inquiry used in workers' education and union work across North America (Hellyer and Schulman, 1989; Schied, 1993), by feminists from the suffragettes onward (Hugo, 1990), and by minorities in their struggle for social justice (Cunningham, 1989). How these groups researched, learned, and made their findings available to others should be a larger part of today's adult education literature (Stubblefield and Keane, 1994).

However, if we move beyond U.S. history, the use of forms of collaborative research, such as participatory research or participatory action research, action research, and transformative research, have been well documented in other countries (Kemmis, 1991; Whitehead, 1989). They have also been documented by international adult educators in developing countries (Deshler, 1991; Fernandes and Tandon, 1981; Hall, Gillette, and Tandon, 1982; Tom and Sork, 1994). The use of participatory action research with indigenous people in countries such as Australia and New Zealand has been documented (McTaggart, 1991). And, at the levels of the United Nations and international agencies, action research has been used and documented extensively for improving health, environmental, and agriculture standards worldwide in African, Caribbean, and Latin American countries (Deshler, 1991; Whyte, 1991).

However, despite the rich history of social reformists and nontraditional adult education in the United States and adult educators around the globe, "legitimate knowledge" from "acceptable research methods" as defined by academics in the professional tradition has dominated the mainstream of the U.S. field (Cervero, 1991).

It is only recently that assumptions about research have begun to change in adult education in ways that allow collaborative methods of research, such as action research, to be deemed acceptable. With the stage beginning to be set for such change in the formal arena of this field, it is instructive to see how forms of collaborative research have evolved in the K–12 system.

Action Research in the Public Education System

A broad challenge to the formal knowledge production process began in public school classrooms in the late 1940s with the seminal work of Kurt Lewin, who in turn was influenced by the work of John Dewey (Peters and Robinson,

1984). At that time, some of the earliest research efforts of public school teachers were in reaction to the rigid scientism of the period (Holly, 1991; McKernan, 1987; Tikunoff and Ward, 1983). However, this nascent action research movement declined in the late 1950s due to academic experts' growing criticism of its "neglect of the traditional scientific method and its lack of methodological rigor" (Catelli, 1995, p. 27).

Interest in action research was rekindled in public schools by Robert Schefer's 1967 book *The School as a Center of Inquiry,* which recommended the use of action-oriented collaboration among teachers for mutual learning and production of knowledge (Catelli, 1995). Bruce Joyce (1972) furthered this type of interest with his laboratory school for the preparation of teachers at Columbia Teachers College (now extant in The Holmes Group, 1990). In the 1970s, interest in action research accelerated with the work of Tikunoff, Ward, and Griffin (1979) and that of Griffin, Lieberman, and Jacullo-Noto (1983). Above all, according to David Kember and Lyn Gow, "revival of interest and wider adoption in the educational arena is largely attributed to the work of Stenhouse, who advanced the idea of teachers as researchers" (1992, p. 297; see also Stenhouse, 1975).

With education leaders in Britain and Australia also taking a keen interest in action research (Bryant and Usher, 1986; Whitehead, 1989), the movement has since grown to form a growing counterhegemony to traditional teacher preparation programs in public education and, more important for this discussion, to traditional scientific positivism and the academic control of knowledge (Kyle and Hovda, 1987; Nixon, 1987).

Action Research and Gradual Change in Traditional Adult Education

As mentioned earlier, the social reformist tradition in adult education has been attempting to influence the professional tradition both at the practice level (for example, Cunningham, 1989) and at the research level for years (Cervero, 1991). Flashpoints over research have occurred, such as that between Budd Hall and William Griffith in 1979. Hall argued from his third world participatory research background. He argued, "We have come dangerously close to creating a situation in the social sciences which effectively denies recognition of the knowledge-creating abilities in most of the peoples of the world" (1979, p. 46). Griffith, at the University of British Columbia, dismissed participatory research as mere problem solving, retorting, "'participatory research' is a misnomer, applied idiosyncratically to activities not conducted primarily to advance knowledge but rather to promote community development" (1979, p. 18). Participatory research, from Griffith's viewpoint, was merely "experimentation without control groups" (p. 32).

Such early debates have probably done more to push the two adult education traditions apart along the ideological divide than they have helped to find common ground. While the differing methodologies of the two camps have typically been on the banner, the ideologies of the researchers have been the real reason for the skirmishes in the field.

Nevertheless, adult education has slowly moved away from a dependence on quantitative research. From the 1950s through the 1970s, "research" in academe typically meant that which the sciences—the social sciences particularly—deemed legitimate through the scientific method and hypothesis testing (Wilson, 1992). Today, Garrison and Shale (1994) review the history of arguments over quantitative versus qualitative research in light of "implicit socio-political agendas" (1994, p. 17) and arrive at the conclusion that "greater efforts need to be made [in adult education] to reconcile seemingly diverse methodologies and findings or, more important, to design research projects that include different methodologies studying the same problem in order that a better understanding may be achieved through a dialectical process" (p. 34).

The shift to greater inclusion of methods and approaches since the late 1970s can be seen in Table 1.1 (see also Deshler and Hagan, 1989).

A review of the Adult Education Research Conference proceedings since they were first published in the late 1950s reveals that challenges to empirical quantitative research began during the late 1960s. Qualitative methods such as case study, grounded theory, ethnography, and phenomenology began to find their way into the research throughout the 1970s and into the 1980s (Deshler and Hagan, 1989, p. 150). Ed Taylor's study of the types of research published in *Adult Education Quarterly* (1993) supports the observation that there has been a shift from quantitative to qualitative since the 1970s (Peters and Banks, 1982). More recently, the introduction of critical theory (Cunningham, 1989), research challenges from feminist researchers, (Hugo, 1990), the exponential rise of ethnographic research, and the "celebration of plurality" with postmodernism

Table 1.1. Research Trends and Coming Challenges

Research Categories				
Natural or "Hard" Sciences	History	Social Sciences	Philosophy	Arts and Social Sciences
Experimental Quasi-experimental Descriptive	Historical	Ethnographic Case study Grounded theory Futures Collaborative Participatory **Action research**	Phenomenology	Postmodern research Deconstruction Reflexivity
Acceptance and Introduction to Adult Education				
1950s–1980s		Mid 1980s	Late 1980s	1990s and beyond
Locus of Power Shift				
Scientific distance		Increased recognition of "the researched," increased collaboration with practitioners	The challenge to help others strengthen their voices	

(Boshier, 1994, p. 102) have opened the door to critical and alternative research methods. As Roger Boshier put it recently, "In adult education research, as elsewhere, there is no doubt that the postmodern turn has opened space for 'other' voices" (1994, p. 103). Still, an open door does not mean everyone will be eager to walk through it.

The Coming Challenge for Adult Education Research

Deshler and Hagan state that "adult education has come a long way in during the last forty years. The types of issues in dispute today . . . are evidence of vitality and opportunity for research creativity for the future" (1989, p. 162). However, not all see it that way. It is our position in this sourcebook that the future of research in formal adult education must include collaborative methods that involve practitioners. The issue of research and knowledge production is a debate not simply over type of method, but over control of the research agenda of the future and who will have the authority to produce the knowledge we will use and be known for as a field of study and practice. These are questions of power and authority embedded in our history. In our opinion, answering them is the greatest challenge the field of adult education will need to face in the future.

There is an understandable defensiveness seen at the academic level in the face of these challenges. As recently as 1994, Tom and Sork stated, "The production of knowledge [seen as] an exclusive and esoteric activity carried on largely by university-based academics is being challenged on a number of fronts" (1994, p. 40). But, in the same textbook, Adrian Blunt said, "Today researchers must not only present evidence that their projects comply with the tenets and rules of their methodology, they must defend their choice of methodology against the attacks of colleagues armed with the 'methodologically correct' views of their alternative, chosen paradigms" (1994, p. 169). The coming challenge to researcher authority is an uncomfortable one for many adult education academics. As Blunt observed, "university adult education researchers have traditionally experienced a 'Catch-22' situation, with practitioners holding a negative attitude toward research as they have judged the results to have contributed nothing of value to practice, and at the same time the reputation of adult education researchers in the university community has suffered because of their focus on applied research" (1994, p. 184).

Clearly, various academic researchers are responding in different ways to the changing research terrain. Blunt has offered a "hard and soft" set of research paradigms whereby research can be separated. Two levels would exist in our research "by the extent it is linked with conceptual, theoretical, and methodological sources from the 'harder' social science disciplines . . . as compared to the 'softer' disciplines of community development, social work, public health, public administration, training and development, and *education generally*" (1994, p. 200, emphasis added). Garrison has also taken a seemingly conciliatory position, saying, "Adult education's gatekeepers must welcome novice researchers into the research community and provide the guidance and support to ensure their continued contribution to the knowledge base of the field" (1994, p. 214). However, like Blunt, he laments the great amount of applied research found in adult education. Garrison wishes more researchers would focus their "activities to a greater extent on matters of educational concern" (1994, p. 13), meaning basic, not applied research. Calling for more basic research, Garrison says, "Adult educators must critically consider whether essentially noneducation activities and causes in political and social fields are central to the adult education phenomena" (1994, p. 13). Here is the historical ideological division—alive and well.

I would argue that rather than being fearful about the field's "lack of theory and quality research," academic researchers should be fearful of being seen as recalcitrant in not including practitioners in the construction of knowledge. Other social science disciplines are including practitioners; the public education system is far ahead of adult education in this. Most adult educators would argue that adult education is and always has been an applied field with a major emphasis on practice. Collaboration has become one of the touchstones of adult education teaching (Knowles, 1980). Michael Welton has noted that dialogue has been considered one of the defining features of adult education throughout our history (Welton, 1995; Habermas, 1970).

I believe that applied, and especially practitioner-directed, action research should become part of the moral responsibility of serving learners. Research should not be the exclusive right of the academic minority to define and "solve" the problems perceived among the majority. In this vein, Peters (1991) has taken a forward-looking, pragmatic position suggesting that the "central organizing construct" (p. 436) for adult education in academe as well as the "the type of research appropriate to the field" (p. 434) should have everything to do with the functions of the field and the issues it seeks to address. He refers to the "need to identify and focus subject matter" (p. 434) in the development of designs to address needs. Peters seeks to begin with our field's purposes and bring together the two worlds "oriented to university and practice" (p. 435) around mutual concerns, meaning practice issues should precede and determine design issues, including appropriate research methods.

Moving us closer to action research, Tom and Sork (1994) have argued for the inclusion of collaborative research—which would include action research—in academic inquiry. They advocate that "if all those who collaborated in the [research project] were equally involved in both disseminating and applying results, the literature and practice of adult education would be enriched (pp. 53–54). With mounting controversy over research and the control of knowledge production, Deshler rightly personalizes research, and asks, "To whom is the researcher accountable—to academic colleagues . . . , to the institution of higher education, to external funders, to practitioners, to the demands of social and historical circumstances, . . . or to himself or herself?" (1991, p. 413).

If the control and legitimation of research were shared between the researcher and the researched for mutual benefit; if the principles and methods of collaboration were advocated by more academic researchers; if our rich history of knowledge production in the nontraditional arena of adult education were more fully included, it is argued that we would be in a much better position to fulfill our mission in this field and build on the broad foundations of both our professional and our social reform traditions.

Characteristics of Action Research and Where It Fits

Action research can be seen as being located within the family of collaborative research methods. In the public school literature, Catelli (1995) broadly defines collaborative research as "the *combined efforts* of teachers, researchers, and teacher educators to engage in a systematic and *'critically' oriented process* of inquiry, in order to understand and improve some *commonly agreed-upon* dimensions of educational practice" (p. 27, emphasis added). The collaborative approaches to research take seriously the role of all participants. Nor do collaborative research approaches seek to be "neutral." Irrespective of the question to be researched, collaborative approaches take a critically oriented and interpretive stance toward what exists (Kemmis, 1991). These approaches begin with the practitioner and what Okunrotifa referred to as "a feeling of dissatisfaction" (1971, p. 155; see also Quigley, 1995). From here, as Kemmis explains, "the researcher aims to *develop* or *improve* people's actions, understandings and situations through collaborative action" (1991, p. 61). Quite different from positivistic research, they "involve the 'subjects' of research as active agents in shaping and interpreting the research" (Tom and Sork, 1994, p. 40). Collaborative approaches begin with a critical assessment of what is and seek through mutual collaborative action to improve some aspect of the group's or a group member's perceived condition (Liston and Zeichner, 1990).

However, beyond the common principles under the umbrella of collaborative research, the family of methods and labels becomes confusing, especially in the K–12 literature. In the public school literature, Clift, Veal, Johnson, and Holland (1990) say collaborative research includes "interactive research and development, clinical inquiry, collaborative staff development research, and collaborative action research" (p. 53). Yet terms found under the collaborative research umbrella also run from *participatory action research* (Whyte, 1991) to *collaborative action research* (Clift, Veal, Johnson, and Holland, 1990) to *collaborative inquiry* (Catelli, 1995). Despite the nomenclature, a widely used term depicting many of these is still *action research* (Lytle and Cochran-Smith, 1990).

Kurt Lewin (1948) described action research as consisting of four distinct steps: planning, executing, reconnaissance, and evaluating (Kember and Gow, 1992). Today, Stephen Kemmis and Robin McTaggart (1984, 1988) are among the best known proponents of action research. They have defined it as follows: "Action research is a form of collective self-reflective inquiry undertaken by participants in a social situation in order to improve the rationality and justice of their own social practices, as well as their understanding of these practices and the situations in which these practices are carried out" (1988, p. 5). However, while the methodologies under the collaborative umbrella have much in common and many seem to be well described by the term *action research,* to imply that all who use it in education are working for the same ends or out of the same philosophic purpose would be an error.

Kemmis has stated that *"critical reflection and self-reflection"* (1991, p. 60) are inherent to action research. They have also argued strongly for an emancipatory purpose for action research. Kemmis, an Australian educator and researcher, states that "there is an interest in *emancipating* people from constraints of irrationality, injustice, oppression and suffering which disfigures their lives, and developing the sense that, as both the products and producers of history, they share circumstances which they can act together to challenge and to change" (1991, p. 60). Meanwhile, the majority of public school action research advocates in the United States clearly take a less radical, more functional position in their understanding and application of action research. This second, much larger group confines Kemmis and McTaggart's "critical reflection" to the classroom and the educational institution and appears to ignore social issues. A review of the literature reveals that the majority of public school teachers do not include communities or societal issues in their understanding of action research. The Kemmis and McTaggart Australian version of action research is what we in adult education will call *participatory research,* as will be seen in Chapters Four and Five.

The institutional change group of public school action researchers has turned to the action science literature of Argyris and others (for example, Argyris, 1982; Argyris and Schön, 1974; Schön, 1983) for their intellectual base, as has an emerging stream in adult education (Cervero, 1988; Brooks and Watkins, 1994b). This school has grounded its work in the professional development literature of reflexivity and reflective practice—as have the action research contributors to this sourcebook.

What differs in both public and adult education is not so much the method or the applications of research, but the depth of social and structural critique that the researchers want to engage in. In this respect, we agree with Kember and Gow (1992, p. 301), that "practical action research can be a *stepping stone* towards *emancipatory* action research" (emphasis added). Because of this, we are hopeful that the mainstream of adult education will continue toward greater acceptance of collaborative principles in research and come to accept institution-based, professional action research as discussed here more widely as the next step for developing practical research knowledge. Some practitioners using action research will move to emancipatory research methods, such as participatory or transformative research; others will not. Some will move on to positivist methods; others will not. We hope that many in academe will accept action research as a viable research method, and we hope this acceptance will be a stepping stone for acceptance of forms of more emancipatory research in the literature.

History shows that change comes incrementally in adult education. A framework that may help us through the coming challenging steps is presented in the next section.

Defining, Framing, and "Locating" Action Research

Unlike the public school literature, adult education has distinguished quite clearly between action research and participatory research in adult education (for example, Merriam and Simpson, 1984; Brooks and Watkins, 1994b). For action research, Sharan Merriam and Ed Simpson echo Lewin by referring to the four steps of action research: "analysis, getting facts, identifying the problem, planning and taking action on the problem, then repeating the cycle as new concepts and information result from the process" (p. 108). This brief description sets action research in the institutional and staff development context, with the attendant reflective practitioner and action science literature (Schön, 1983; Argyris, 1982; Argyris and Schön, 1974).

By contrast, the version of collaborative inquiry termed *participatory research,* as referred to by Hall earlier, or *participatory action research* (Miller, 1994), as it is called by many in popular education (Torres and Fischman, 1994), takes "a broader perspective of the term 'problem'" (Merriam and Simpson, 1984, p. 108). Participatory research has been described as "the political empowerment of people through group participation research in the search for and acquisition of knowledge" (Merriam and Simpson, 1984 p. 108). Therefore, unlike the K–12 literature, which tends to blur action research and participatory research—at least in the U.S. context—it has been clearly stated in the adult education literature that the entire area of participatory research "has empowerment and human equality as its aim" (Merriam and Simpson, 1984, p. 108). Tom and Sork (1994) expand the discussion by aligning transformative research with participatory research—both for emancipatory purposes. They cite Deshler and Selener in describing transformative research, as follows: "Transformative is 'not a new research methodology, but a particular philosophical stance. . . . That stance . . . is one that views the focus, the process, and the outcomes of research as the means by which confrontation and action against the causes of injustice, exploitation, violence, and environmental degradation can occur through the research process and the use of research results'" (Tom and Sork, 1994, p. 41).

The distinctions among these variations of collaborative research have been discussed by Brooks and Watkins (1994b). However, neither Merriam and Simpson, nor Tom and Sork, nor Brooks and Watkins discuss the deeper ideological differences between emancipatory participatory or transformative research and the practical/professional action research to be discussed here.

Many have tried to develop a framework for adult education research approaches (see Deshler and Hagan, 1989; Brooks and Watkins, 1994a, 1994b). Given adult education's history and the importance of ideology as discussed here, I suggest that a framework for adult education that includes types of collaborative research available may be drawn from the early work of the philosopher Jürgen Habermas. In his work, Habermas has asserted that individuals construct their own knowledge and provide meanings for that knowledge. In the 1970s, Habermas said there are three distinct knowledge-constitutive interests at work in the social construction of knowledge: technical, practical, and emancipatory interests (Habermas, 1970; see also Kember and Gow, 1992) (see Table 1.2). The basis for framing research, in this context, is the researcher's interest, or more exactly, the researcher's intent.

For purposes of this discussion, "technical" might be seen to embrace positivist methods such as experimental and quasi-experimental research. The methods involved work to keep the object and subject of research quite separate and impose as little communicative interaction as possible between the two. The researcher enters the research with no asserted intentional purpose other than a stated technical study of testing hypotheses through deductive reasoning. Through careful control of the environment, the methods in this technical category promise generalizability. Neither the researcher nor the researched assume immediate practicality. As Kerlinger put it some years ago, "the *basic* aim of science is not the betterment of mankind. It is theory. . . . Other aims of science . . . are: explanation, understanding, prediction, and control" (1973, p. 9). The professional tradition of adult education discussed earlier has subscribed to this scientific rationality, or technical approach, for its knowledge base since the 1930s (Wilson, 1992).

To continue with Habermas, the "practical" category can be seen as including the interpretive realm of research methods for practical change. This type of research would include reflectivity and action science for, especially, practitioner development and institutional improvement. It typically seeks and intends to improve criticality. It typically intends to close the gap between theory and practice. In short, the practical category of research typically intends to provide outcomes that have an application immediately related to the practice world of the individuals involved.

Table 1.2. A Research Intentionality Framework for Adult Education

	Technical	*Practical*	*Emancipatory*
Goal	To understand and generalize	To understand or improve	To understand and redress
Nature	Deductive	Inductive	Inductive
Type	Empirical	Interpretive on an individual or group basis	Interpretive on a group basis
Approach	Control	Observe or collaborate	Interact
Method	Experimental Quasi-experimental Descriptive	Grounded theory Transformative Case study Phenomenology Ethnography Historical	

Action research   **Participatory research**

Collaborative

The research methods to be included here would be action research, case study, grounded theory, ethnographic research, futures research, and, in many instances, phenomenological research. The approaches range from group/researcher collaboration to deep self-reflection, but all seek as their typical objective to improve the knowledge, functions, or working environment of the self or an immediate group in a self-defined manner through induction. This category of research does not seek the wide generalizability seen earlier in the technical category; nevertheless, the resultant "descriptive accounts of concrete cases can be useful to make extrapolations to different cases" (McTaggart, 1991, p. 169).

The third category, "emancipatory," increases the degree of discourse that is free from nondemocratic restraints—a condition of Habermas's theory of communicative competence (1970). Here the research methods would include community-based participatory research and transformative research for emancipation and human justice. In this category, the goals are to effect social change. Group involvement, not simply individual involvement or group support to an individual, is prerequisite. Likewise, full discourse among all members is expected throughout the research (Cervero, 1991; Merriam and Simpson, 1984). The emancipatory research approach seeks to rectify a situation of oppression, not merely one of dissatisfaction. It seeks to bring structural, or "deep," change in social conditions, not simply institutional improvements (Beder, 1989). Here, political activism and conflict is more than a possibility; its ideology is based on an awareness of conflict and power as well as a keen sensitivity to social injustice. Descriptions of concrete cases and the actions taken can be extrapolated to others in similar conditions—as in the case of groups at Highlander Research and Education Center learning about others' efforts in similar circumstances. In short, The intent of emancipatory research is not generalizability nor practical practitioner or institutional improvement; it seeks increased empowerment and enhanced self-determination.

Research begins with a question and a desire for change. Zora Neale Hurston once wrote, "Research is formalized curiosity. It is poking and prying with purpose. It is a seeking that he who wishes may know the cosmic secrets of the world and they that dwell therein" (1984, p. 174). The action research discussed in this book by the editors and the contributors to the case studies falls within the practical and professional development category of this framework by research intention. The action researchers in the following chapters have poked and pried with the purpose of improving both the practice and the outcomes of adult education in traditional settings. We now turn to the problem-posing, problem-solving specifics of action research in Chapter Two.

References

Adams, F. *Unearthing Seeds of Fire: The Idea of Highlander.* Winston-Salem, N.C.: Blair, 1975.
Alinsky, S. *Rules for Radicals: A Practical Primer for Realistic Radicals.* New York: Random House, 1972.

Argyris, C. *Reasoning, Learning and Action: Individual and Organizational.* San Francisco: Jossey-Bass, 1982.

Argyris, C., and Schön, D. A. *Theory in Practice: Increasing Professional Effectiveness.* San Francisco: Jossey-Bass, 1974.

Beder, H. "Purposes and Philosophies of Adult Education." In S. B. Merriam and P. M. Cunningham (eds.), *Handbook of Adult and Continuing Education.* San Francisco: Jossey-Bass, 1989.

Blunt, A. "The Future of Adult Education Research." In R. Garrison (ed.), *Research Perspectives in Adult Education.* Malabar, Fla.: Krieger, 1994.

Boshier, R. "Initiating Research." In R. Garrison (ed.), *Research Perspectives in Adult Education.* Malabar, Fla.: Krieger, 1994.

Briton, D. *The Modern Practice of Adult Education: A Postmodern Critique.* New York: State University of New York Press, 1996.

Brooks, A., and Watkins, K. E. (eds.). *The Emerging Power of Action Inquiry Technologies.* New Directions for Adult and Continuing Education, no. 63. San Francisco: Jossey-Bass, 1994a.

Brooks, A., and Watkins, K. E. "A New Era for Action Technologies: A Look at the Issues." In A. Brooks and K. E. Watkins (eds.), *The Emerging Power of Action Inquiry Technologies.* New Directions for Adult and Continuing Education, no. 63. San Francisco: Jossey-Bass, 1994b.

Bryant, I., and Usher, R. "Tension Points in Adult Education Research." Paper presented at the annual meeting of the Standing Committee on University Teaching and Research in the Education of Adults, University of Hull, England, June 1986.

Catelli, L. "Action Research and Collaborative Inquiry in a School-University Partnership." *Action in Teacher Education,* 1995, *16* (4), 25–38.

Cervero, R. M. *Effective Continuing Education for Professionals.* San Francisco: Jossey-Bass, 1988.

Cervero, R. "Changing Relationships Between Theory and Practice." In J. M. Peters, P. J. Jarvis, and Associates, *Adult Education: Evolution and Achievements in a Developing Field of Study.* San Francisco: Jossey-Bass, 1991.

Clift, R., Veal, M. L., Johnson, M., and Holland, P. "Restructuring Teacher Education Through Collaborative Action Research." *Journal of Teacher Education,* 1990, *41* (2), 52–62.

Cockley, S. *The Adult Educator's Guide to Practitioner Research.* Dayton: Virginia Adult Educators Research Network, 1993.

Conger, S. *Canadian Open Adult Learning Systems.* Prince Albert, Canada: Department of Manpower and Immigration, 1974.

Cookson, P. "International and Comparative Adult Education." In S. B. Merriam and P. M. Cunningham (eds.), *Handbook of Adult and Continuing Education.* San Francisco: Jossey-Bass, 1989.

Costanza, A. "Participatory Action Research: A View from the ACTWU." In W. F. Whyte (ed.), *Participatory Action Research.* Thousand Oaks, Calif.: Sage, 1991.

Cotton, W. "The Challenge Confronting American Adult Education." *Adult Education,* 1964, *14* (2), 80–87.

Courtney, S. "Defining Adult and Continuing Education." In S. B. Merriam and P. M. Cunningham (eds.), *Handbook of Adult and Continuing Education.* San Francisco: Jossey-Bass, 1989.

Cunningham, P. "Making a Greater Impact on Society." In B. A. Quigley (ed.), *Fulfilling the Promise of Adult and Continuing Education.* New Directions for Continuing Education, no. 44. San Francisco: Jossey-Bass, 1989.

Deshler, D. "Social, Professional, and Academic Issues." In J. M. Peters, P. J. Jarvis, and Associates, *Adult Education: Evolution and Achievements in a Developing Field of Study.* San Francisco: Jossey-Bass, 1991.

Deshler, D., and Hagan, N. "Adult Education Research." In S. B. Merriam and P. M. Cunningham (eds.), *Handbook of Adult and Continuing Education.* San Francisco: Jossey-Bass, 1989.

Fernandes, W., and Tandon, R. *Participatory Research and Evaluation: Experiments in Research as a Process of Liberation.* New Delhi: Indian Social Institute, 1981.

Garrison, R. "Conclusion." In R. Garrison (ed.), *Research Perspectives in Adult Education*. Malabar, Fla.: Krieger, 1994.

Garrison, R., and Shale, D. "Methodological Issues: Philosophical Differences and Complementary Methodologies." In R. Garrison (ed.), *Research Perspectives in Adult Education*. Malabar, Fla.: Krieger, 1994.

Gaventa, J., and Horton, M. "A Citizen's Research Project in Appalachia, USA." *Convergence*, 1981, *14*, 30–42.

Grattan, H. *In Quest of Knowledge*. New York: Association Press, 1955.

Griffin, G., Lieberman, A., and Jacullo-Noto, J. *Interactive Research and Development on Schooling*. Austin: Research and Development Center for Teacher Education, University of Texas, 1983.

Griffith, W. "Participatory Research: Should It Be a New Methodology for Adult Educators?" In J. Niemi (ed.), *Viewpoints on Adult Education Research*. Information Series no. 171. Columbus: ERIC Clearinghouse on Adult, Career, and Vocational Education, Ohio State University, 1979.

Guba, E. G., and Lincoln, Y. S. *Effective Evaluation: Improving the Usefulness of Evaluation Results Through Responsive and Naturalistic Approaches*. San Francisco: Jossey-Bass, 1981.

Habermas, J. "Towards a Theory of Communicative Competence." *Inquiry*, 1970, *13*, 360–375.

Hall, B. "Participatory Research: Breaking the Academic Monopoly." In J. Niemi (ed.), *Viewpoints on Adult Education Research*. Information Series no. 171. Columbus: ERIC Clearinghouse on Adult, Career, and Vocational Education, Ohio State University, 1979.

Hall, B., Gillette, A., and Tandon, R. *Creating Knowledge: A Monopoly? Participatory Research in Development*. Participatory Research Network Series, no. 1. Toronto: International Council for Adult Education, 1982.

Heaney, T. "St. Mary's Community Education Center: Can Alternatives Survive Success?" *Thresholds*, 1977, *3* (3), 18–19.

Hellyer, M., and Schulman, B. "Workers' Education." In S. B. Merriam and P. M. Cunningham (eds.), *Handbook of Adult and Continuing Education*. San Francisco: Jossey-Bass, 1989.

Holly, P. "Action Research: The Missing Link in the Creation of Schools as Centers of Inquiry." In A. Lieberman and L. Miller (eds.), *Staff Development for Education in the '90's*. New York: Teachers College Press, 1991.

Holmes Group, The. *Tomorrow's Schools: Principles for the Design of Professional Development Schools*. East Lansing, Mich.: The Holmes Group, 1990.

Hugo, J. "Adult Education History and the Issue of Gender: Toward a Different History of Adult Education in America." *Adult Education Quarterly*, 1990, *41* (1), 1–16.

Hurston, Z. N. *Dust Tracks on a Road*. Chicago: University of Illinois Press, 1984.

Jensen, G., Liveright, A., and Hallenbeck, W. (eds.). *Adult Education: Outlines of an Emerging Field of University Study*. Washington, D.C.: Adult Education Association of the USA, 1964.

Joyce, B. "The Teacher Innovator: A Program for Preparing Teachers." In B. Joyce and M. Weil (eds.), *Perspectives for Reform in Teacher Education*. Englewood Cliffs, N.J.: Prentice Hall, 1972.

Kember, D., and Gow, L. "Action Research as a Form of Staff Development in Higher Education." *Higher Education*, 1992, *23*, 297–310.

Kemmis, S. "Improving Education Through Action Research." In O. Zuber-Skerritt (ed.), *Action Research for Change and Development*. Brookfield, Vt.: Gower, 1991.

Kemmis, S., and McTaggart, R. (eds.). *The Action Research Planner*. Geelong, Australia: Deakin University Press, 1984.

Kemmis, S., and McTaggart, R. (eds.). *The Action Research Planner*. (2nd ed.) Geelong, Australia: Deakin University Press, 1988.

Kerlinger, F. *Foundations of Behavioral Research*. (2nd ed.) Austin, Tex.: Holt, Rinehart and Winston, 1973.

Knowles, M. *The Modern Practice of Adult Education*. (2nd ed.) New York: Cambridge Books, 1980.

Kyle, D., and Hovda, R. "Action Research: Comments on Current Trends and Future Possibilities." *Peabody Journal of Education,* 1987, *64* (3), 170–175.

Lewin, K. *Resolving Social Conflicts.* New York: HarperCollins, 1948.

Liston, D., and Zeichner, K. "Reflective Teaching and Action Research in Preservice Teacher Education." *Journal of Education for Teaching,* 1990, *16* (3), 235–253.

Lowe, J. *The Education of Adults: A World Perspective.* (2nd ed.) Toronto: Ontario Institute for Studies in Education, 1975.

Lytle, S., and Cochran-Smith, M. "Learning from Teacher Research: A Working Typology." *Teachers College Record,* 1990, *92* (1), 83–103.

McDonald, B. "Director's Column." *The Community Exchange,* 1994, 2 (4), 2.

McKernan, J. "Action Research and Curriculum Development." *Peabody Journal of Education,* 1987, *64* (2), 6–19.

McTaggart, R. "Principles for Participatory Action Research." *Adult Education Quarterly,* 1991, *41* (3), 168–187.

Merriam, S. "How Research Produces Knowledge." In J. M. Peters, P. J. Jarvis, and Associates, *Adult Education: Evolution and Achievements in a Developing Field of Study.* San Francisco: Jossey-Bass, 1991.

Merriam, S., and Simpson, E. *A Guide to Research for Educators and Trainers of Adults.* Malabar, Fla.: Krieger, 1984.

Miller, N. "Participatory Action Research: Principles, Politics, and Possibilities." In A. Brooks and K. E. Watkins (eds.), *The Emerging Power of Action Inquiry Technologies.* New Directions for Adult and Continuing Education, no. 63. San Francisco: Jossey-Bass, 1994.

Nixon, J. "The Teacher as Researcher: Contradictions and Continuities." *Peabody Journal of Education,* 1987, *64* (2), 20–32.

Okunrotifa, P. "Curriculum Improvement Through Action Research." *Teacher Education in New Countries,* 1971, *12* (2), 153–161.

Pace, L., and Argona, D. "Participatory Action Research: A View from Xerox." In W. F. Whyte (ed.), *Participatory Action Research.* Thousand Oaks, Calif.: Sage, 1991.

Pates, A. "Collaborative Research in ABE." *Vision,* 1992, *4* (2), 1, 3–4.

Peters, J. "Advancing the Study of Adult Education." In J. M. Peters, P. J. Jarvis, and Associates, *Adult Education: Evolution and Achievements in a Developing Field of Study.* San Francisco: Jossey-Bass, 1991.

Peters, J., and Banks, B. "Adult Education." In H. E. Mitzel (ed.), *Encyclopedia of Education.* (5th ed.) New York: Free Press, 1982.

Peters, M., and Robinson, V. "The Origins and Status of Action Research." *Journal of Applied Behavioral Science,* 1984, *20* (2), 113–124.

Quigley, A. "Trials, Traditions and the Twenty-First Century." *Adult Learning,* 1991, 3 (2), 21–22, 27.

Quigley, A. *Pennsylvania Action Research Handbook and Project Planner.* Harrisburg: Pennsylvania Department of Education, 1995.

Quigley, A., Dean, G., and Lawson, P. "The Protection of Human Subjects: Possibilities and Problems in Adult Education Research." In G. Dean and T. Ferro (eds.), *Proceedings of the Pennsylvania Adult and Continuing Education Research Conference.* Indiana, Pa.: Indiana University of Pennsylvania, 1994.

Rose, A. "Beyond Classroom Walls: The Carnegie Association and the Founding of the American Association for Adult Education." *Adult Education Quarterly,* 1989, *39* (3), 140–151.

Rubenson, K. "The Sociology of Adult Education." In S. B. Merriam and P. M. Cunningham (eds.), *Handbook of Adult and Continuing Education.* San Francisco: Jossey-Bass, 1989.

Schied, F. *Learning in Social Context: Workers and Adult Education in Nineteenth Century Chicago.* DeKalb: LEPS Press, Northern Illinois University, 1993.

Schön, D. *The Reflective Practitioner.* New York: Basic Books, 1983.

Shafer, C. "Doing Research with Communities: Smart Research That Results in Sustainable Change." *Innovations in Community and Rural Development,* Dec. 1995, pp. 1–2.

Stenhouse, L. *Introduction to Curriculum Research and Development.* Portsmouth, N.H.: Heinemann, 1975.

Stubblefield, H. W., and Keane, P. *Adult Education in the American Experience: From the Colonial Period to the Present.* San Francisco: Jossey-Bass, 1994.

Taylor, E. "Gatekeeping and the AEQ: An Inside View." *34th Annual Adult Education Research Conference.* University Park: Pennsylvania State University, 1993.

Tikunoff, W., and Ward, B. "Collaborative Research on Teaching." *Elementary School Journal,* 1983, *83,* 453–468.

Tikunoff, W., Ward, B., and Griffin, G. *Interactive Research and Development on Teaching Study: Final Report.* San Francisco: Far West Regional Laboratory for Educational Research and Development, 1979.

Tom, A., and Sork, T. "Issues in Collaborative Research." In R. Garrison (ed.), *Research Perspectives in Adult Education.* Malabar, Fla.: Krieger, 1994.

Torbert, W. "Why Educational Research Has Been So Uneducational: The Case for a New Model of Social Science Based on Collaborative Inquiry." In P. Reason and J. Rowan (eds.), *Human Inquiry: A Sourcebook of New Paradigm Research.* New York: Wiley, 1981.

Torres, C. A., and Fischman, G. "Popular Education: Building from Experience." In A. Brooks and K. E. Watkins (eds.), *The Emerging Power of Action Inquiry Technologies.* New Directions for Adult and Continuing Education, no. 63. San Francisco: Jossey-Bass, 1994.

Tough, A. *The Adult's Learning Projects: A Fresh Approach to Theory and Practice on Adult Education.* (2nd ed.) Toronto: Ontario Institute for Studies in Education, 1971.

van Manen, M. "Beyond Assumptions: Shifting the Limits of Action Research." *Theory into Practice,* 1990, *29* (3), 153–157.

Verner, C., and Booth, A. *Adult Education.* Washington, D.C.: Center for Applied Research in Education, 1964.

Weisbord, M. R. *Productive Workplaces: Organizing and Managing for Dignity, Meaning, and Community.* San Francisco: Jossey-Bass, 1987.

Welton, M. *In Defense of the Lifeworld: Critical Perspectives on Adult Learning.* Albany: State University of New York Press, 1995.

Whitehead, J. "How Do We Improve Research-Based Professionalism in Education? A Question Which Includes Action Research, Educational Theory and the Politics of Educational Knowledge." *British Educational Journal,* 1989, *15* (1), 3–17.

Whyte, W. F. (ed.). *Participatory Action Research.* Thousand Oaks, Calif.: Sage, 1991.

Wilson, A. "Science and the Professionalization of American Adult Education, 1934–1989: A Study of Knowledge Development in the Adult Education Handbooks." In A. Blunt (ed.), *Proceedings of the 33rd Annual Adult Education Research Conference.* Saskatoon, Canada: University of Saskatchewan, 1992.

B. ALLAN QUIGLEY is associate professor and regional director of adult education at Pennsylvania State University and director of the Pennsylvania Action Research Network.

Action research as a method of problem posing and problem solving is explained, with suggestions for developing an action research project. The cycles of action research and the questions needed to operationalize the approach are discussed.

Understanding and Using Action Research in Practice Settings

Gary W. Kuhne, B. Allan Quigley

As seen in the previous chapter, action research is a form of inductive, practical research that focuses on gaining a better understanding of a practice problem or achieving a real change or improvement in the practice context. In brief summary, action research, as an approach to research, is essentially a systematic process of practitioner problem posing and problem solving. In carrying out this systematic process of problem posing and problem solving, action research uses a kind of trial-and-error approach when seeking to both understand and resolve practice-based problems and issues. Action research can partially be understood as a process of trial and error because when using this research strategy, an adult education practitioner-researcher tries a hunch or intervention, then, after observing and reflecting on the outcomes, typically tries yet another variation of the intervention (Argyris, 1982). Yet action research is much more than merely trial and error, because it incorporates systematic procedures that combine analysis, observation, and data collection into the process. The systematic use of analysis, observation, and data collection procedures gives action research the potential to achieve useful answers to practice problems. Further, action research also has the potential of having its findings applied in similar practice settings across the country.

We gratefully acknowledge the funding and professional support provided by the Pennsylvania Department of Education, Bureau of Adult Basic and Literacy Education. This support helped create the Pennsylvania Action Research Network discussed in Chapter Five and the Pennsylvania Handbook and Project Planner, where many of the concepts discussed in this text originated.

As seen in the previous chapter, a great frustration for adult educators is the fact that practice problems seldom seem to bear much resemblance to the problems and issues addressed by the professional researchers in higher education institutions. Action research directly addresses such a frustration because it is an approach to research that is designed to be carried out by practitioners in the actual practice setting. Action research is an approach that allows adult education practitioners to both improve their practice and better understand the nature of that practice.

The distinctions are perhaps best summarized by Kemmis and McTaggart (1984) in their discussion of action research, where they describe it as an open, ongoing process based on putting new ideas to the test: "[Action research involves] trying new ideas in practice as a means of improvement and as a means of increasing knowledge about the curriculum, teaching, and learning. The result is improvement in what happens in the classroom and school, and a better articulation and justification of the educational rationale for what goes on. Action research provides a way of working which links theory and practice into the one whole: ideas-in-action" (p. 5). We think that "articulation and justification of the educational rationale for what goes on" is the key phrase here, since the results of action research can build the basis for an argument for change, including a case for increased funds or program structural changes. Such outcomes hold a pragmatic promise for practitioners faced with the ever-present challenge of justifying and improving adult education programs.

Core Processes in Action Research

As seen in the previous chapter, John Dewey's emphasis on reflexive thinking and Kurt Lewin's use of action research provided early perspectives on the nature of action research. Based on their theories, action research can be understood as an approach to problem posing and problem solving that proceeds through four distinct processes: planning, acting, observing, and reflecting. These four basic processes in turn create a cycle of research efforts. Once a practitioner-researcher progresses through these four processes, the cycle of research, he or she will often decide to try yet another cycle of the four processes (revising the plan, acting, observing, and reflecting). In fact, action research often leads to multiplied cycles of problem posing and problem solving that progressively enable adult educators to successfully address the issues and problems in their institutions. These core processes, rooted in Dewey and Lewin, are illustrated in Figure 2.1.

The ability to both accurately understand and effectively intervene in practice problems is an essential competency for all adult educators. Action research, with its emphasis on problem posing and problem solving, offers a practical tool for professional development of adult educators. As adult educators develop increasing proficiency with the action research process, they also develop the skills necessary to begin to solve the many ill-defined and unique problems that form the nature of practice realities (Houle, 1980; Cervero, 1988; Schön, 1983).

Figure 2.1. Four Core Processes of Action Research

Key: Responding to practice problems through problem posing and problem solving

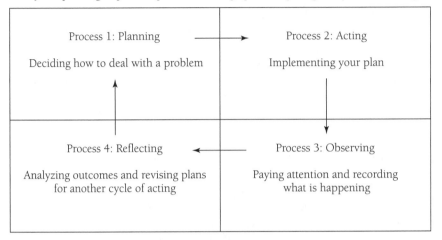

Thus training in action research skills holds great promise for the effective continuing professional development of adult educators in various settings.

Since action research encourages an ongoing cycle of interventions that progressively define and solve practice problems, in one sense action research never really ends. Since practice problems seldom remain static, solutions cannot either. The adult educator who employs action research to address problems in his or her practice will find the development of useful knowledge an increasingly normal part of the work experience. Since one cycle of action research tends to bridge into other cycles of research on the same or similar problems, it often provides the practitioner with a means to test new insights as they appear and to observe systematically how each of these new insights affects practice.

So how does an adult educator begin to incorporate action research into his or her attempts to solve practice problems? First, the adult educator (volunteer, teacher, program planner, administrator, counselor, or policymaker) must gain a good grasp of the actual problem before he or she can systematically intervene to solve it. Interestingly, getting such a grasp of the essence of the true problem is the most difficult part of the action research process. In other words, problem posing is a difficult but necessary first step to problem solving.

Trying to identify a manageable (that is, researchable) problem is the first stage in the planning phase of action research. The difficulty of problem posing is rooted in the fact that, typically, problems in professional practice are like the layers of an onion; when you remove one layer, you find there is another right below it. Experience has shown that problem posing is greatly assisted when practitioners dialogue with other practitioners familiar with the issue being raised. Such dialogue and brainstorming often will provide insights that help the practitioner. Beyond such dialogue, spending time to gather additional facts about the perceived problem can help the practitioner better understand the true nature of the practice-based concern. A combination of fact-finding and dialogue with fellow practitioners should help to clarify the problem enough to begin problem solving.

Of course, action research may not be the best approach to studying a problem once you begin to understand the true nature of the issues involved. For instance, action research may be a very good way to study a new math technique and compare it with an old technique. Action research can also be a good way to study a new counseling strategy to improve retention across a set of courses, or to see if a new recruitment approach is better than the old one. On the other hand, action research likely will not help in trying to study or resolve very emotionally charged or complex political issues such as personal difficulties on the job with an insensitive supervisor. Action research is not a good choice for dealing with a faltering program located in a neighborhood hostile to the adult educator's presence. Some practice-based problems are so psychologically, emotionally, or politically charged that they require more than an action research study to either fully understand or change them. (For further discussion, see Chapter One and Chapter Five.)

Understanding the need to fit the method to the problem is important. How does one decide what sort of problem is appropriate for an action research approach? In addition to the limitations identified in the previous paragraph, two rules of thumb can be used: (1) Take on only what you can personally manage and carry through on. Remember, the advice and ongoing support of colleagues is usually key to a successful project. (2) Begin with a small aspect of a identified problem. Then, as you go, decide what the next intervention should be in a later cycle to resolve the problem. Overall, build answers through small, well-understood steps.

In the next section we will examine the practical steps in action research at each phase in the process. Understanding such steps will help you implement an action research strategy in the context of your own practice-based problems.

Implementing Action Research: Six Steps

As we have already seen, action research is a form of inductive experimentation that follows a process of planning, acting, observing, and reflecting. These processes in turn create a cycle of research that often leads to other cycles. These cycles are created as one moves through a set of decisions and sequential steps in the first cycle; then, having learned something from this first cycle, one typically tries a revised intervention through a second cycle. Unlike many other research methods, action research by its very nature typically demands revision, refinement, and redefinition of the problem itself because it is conducted in the changing world of practice. In this sourcebook, we conceive of the cycle of action research as a process that builds out of six systematic steps that occur during the three distinct phases of the problem-posing and problem-solving process (Quigley, 1995). Figure 2.2 illustrates the cycle of action research, with its phases and steps.

For the sake of simplifying the action research process, we see it as a cycle of problem posing and problem solving that goes through three phases in each cycle of research: a planning phase, an action phase, and a reflection phase. Taken together, these phases, with the specific steps included in each phase, create the cycle of action research. Let's examine these phases and the steps contained within each phase.

Cycle One: Planning Phase. The motivation to try a project usually resides in what we call an "itch." The itch originates from something we do, something we experience, something we become aware of that we just cannot

Figure 2.2. Cycles of Action Research

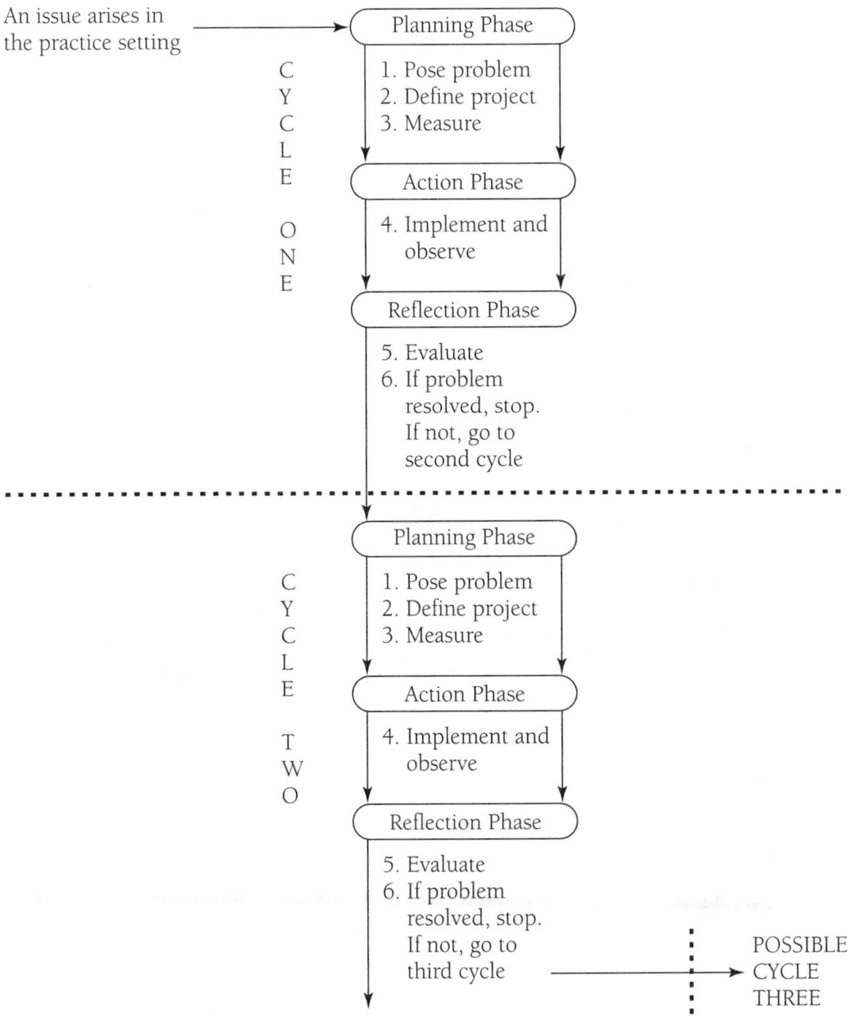

An issue arises in
the practice setting

C
Y
C
L
E

O
N
E

Planning Phase

1. Pose problem
2. Define project
3. Measure

Action Phase

4. Implement and
   observe

Reflection Phase

5. Evaluate
6. If problem
   resolved, stop.
   If not, go to
   second cycle

C
Y
C
L
E

T
W
O

Planning Phase

1. Pose problem
2. Define project
3. Measure

Action Phase

4. Implement and
   observe

Reflection Phase

5. Evaluate
6. If problem
   resolved, stop.
   If not, go to
   third cycle

POSSIBLE
CYCLE
THREE

seem to make "work," yet we know it *should* work. In our opinion, it is the superior practitioners who step forward at this very point because they see practice-based problems as a personal challenge rather than simply something to either complain about or try to ignore. In fact, rather than being frustrated, the risk takers-those who express their commitment with action-try to visualize ways to do something about the perceived problem. They try to envision possibilities for solving problems; they look at solutions others have tried and consider how such solutions would work in their own practice setting. By reviewing others' research on the same or similar problems, they try to imagine how to change their situation. Such research, envisioning, and comparing is the first and probably the most challenging step in the planning phase. But it is also the step that leads to new knowledge and ultimately to more effectiveness for all practitioners. The three phases and the six steps of the action research cycle are illustrated in Figure 2.3.

Figure 2.3. Phases and Steps of Action Research

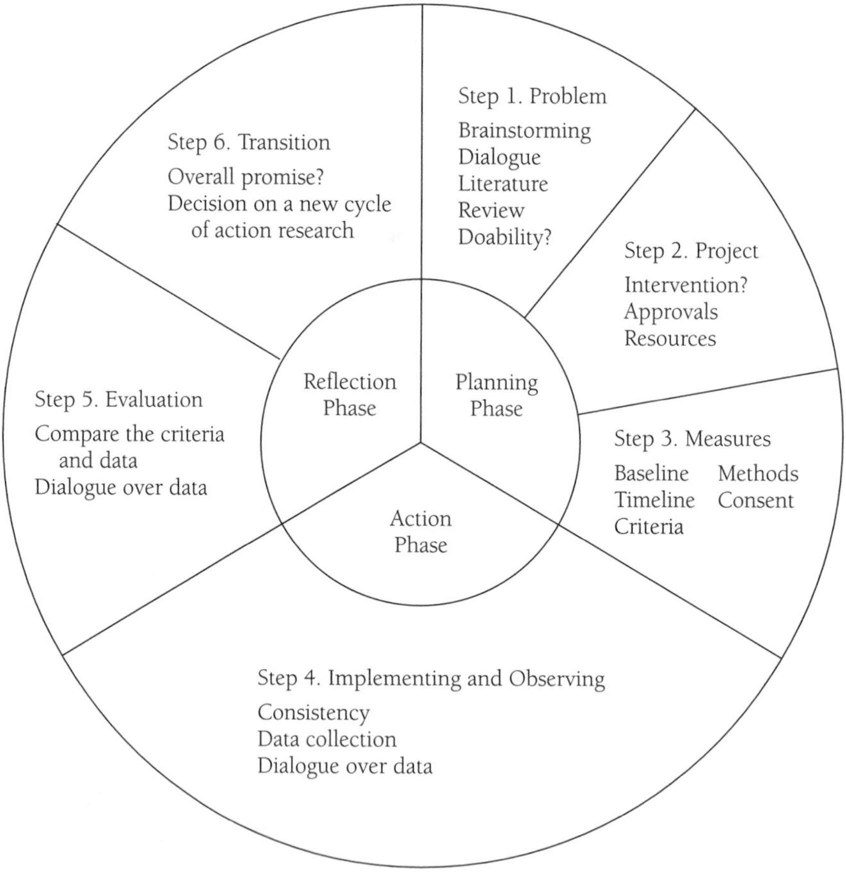

Step 6. Transition
Overall promise?
Decision on a new cycle
of action research

Step 1. Problem
Brainstorming
Dialogue
Literature
Review
Doability?

Step 2. Project
Intervention?
Approvals
Resources

Step 5. Evaluation
Compare the criteria
and data
Dialogue over data

Reflection
Phase

Planning
Phase

Step 3. Measures
Baseline   Methods
Timeline   Consent
Criteria

Action
Phase

Step 4. Implementing and Observing
Consistency
Data collection
Dialogue over data

Step One: Understanding the Problem. Step one in the cycle of action research begins, therefore, with trying to identify the actual problem and deciding where and how to intervene in the problem. This step may take some time to clarify, and it often involves brainstorming as one thinks through some of the intervention options with others knowledgeable on the issue, perhaps colleagues or a mentor. This step may also involve searching the professional literature to see what has been done on similar issues; for adult educators this usually means a search of the ERIC database at a local university or public library (Mekosh-Rosenbaum, n.d.).

After brainstorming and searching, and before moving ahead with the action research, it is important to decide if the problem is both "researchable" and significant for one's own work. Is it "solvable," and is it going to be worth the effort? If you decide your problem or issue is actually researchable, significant, solvable, and worthwhile, you can begin to clarify your intervention through the following key questions: What actually is the problem? Do you understand why the problem exists? How do others see it? Do you have any initial ideas on how to intervene?

Several issues need to be understood at this point in the action research cycle. First, it is not uncommon for the practitioner to have to face the possibility that he or she is part of the problem. Second, it is not uncommon for the process of defining of the actual problem to take quite a bit of time. Some action researchers discovered that it took months to gather facts and determine the problem they wanted to work on. In one example, related in the case studies of action research in Chapter Three, a nurse-trainer working in an intensive care unit in a hospital needed to keep a log for weeks. The minister's case study in Chapter Three involved forming an ad hoc committee to collect information and decide on the best intervention.

Getting the problem and the intervention straight is critical to a successful outcome. Try to involve a sympathetic but informed friend or colleague as you try to figure out the problem and your best-hunch intervention. As an example of the process, consider an action research project Allan undertook with his Introduction to Adult Education course (the first class most returning adult graduates take for their Adult Education degree at our university). In the past Allan had asked students to read several chapters or articles in preparation for the discussion at the following week's class—a classic approach to teaching seminar-style classes. First students would read, then meet to discuss. However, many students complained that there was too much reading. Worse, they did very little discussing. Allan ended up lecturing instead of fostering a discussion. Deciding he did not want to teach this graduate class in a lecture fashion, Allan felt an "itch" that lent itself to an action research solution.

What was the real problem in this graduate course? Many of the students argued that the real problem was the amount of reading. Yet when Allan cut down on the reading assignments, there was little difference in the classroom experience. It was always "too much" no matter how much was dropped. Then one of the students suggested that Allan present a brief lecture on the topic for the next week—in effect, that he use a mini-lecture as an advance organizer. Initially Allan found this suggested solution somewhat uncomfortable, since it implied the problem had more to do with his effectiveness as a teacher than with the students as capable learners. It meant lecturing, which he wanted to avoid. After more reflection, however, he decided to experiment with the mini-lecture approach in the next semester, to discover whether the discussion would flow better from such a teaching practice. He spent the time to define the problem and develop an intervention.

Step Two: Defining the Project. After conceptualizing the practice problem, you are ready for the next step in the planning phase, in which you define in more detail how to organize the intervention and make a change in the problem. Without being clear about the nature of the actual problem, it would be foolish to think in terms of an intervention. In addition, thinking about a possible intervention without also spending the necessary time to develop a fully supported plan of action will inevitably lead to failure. Some questions will arise as you try to organize any intervention for solving a practice-based problem: How can you intervene with a new strategy to see if it would make a difference? When and how should you begin the project? How will you inform or involve participants in the project? Whose approval will you need? Will you need any resources or other personal preparation? Answering these questions will provide the necessary structure and support to implement an intervention. Such questions help researchers to be both realistic and organized in their action research projects.

Let's see how this process worked in the example of using mini-lectures in Allan's graduate course. Allan did decide to try the mini-lecture. He decided to tell the class about the change and get their input as to which teaching method they liked best after a two-month trial period. After gaining assurance from students that no one objected, Allan proceeded with the action research project. The first month involved the old discussion method; the second month involved the mini-lecture approach. After the second month, it would be time for the midterm test. For the second month, Allan prepared succinct mini-lectures on the highlights and issues of the next week's readings. He also gave a written synopsis of the material and some discussion questions to consider. After this, he was ready to consider the data collection techniques.

Step Three: Determining the Measures. If you are to have a sense of whether something is "better," you need to know where you started. "Better" involves a comparison or a value judgment: better compared to what? Unlike daily teaching or administration, in which you can simply try something, action research requires that you take the time to evaluate what you are doing and create a documented comparison based on the results. The intervention you are considering, you hope, will bring about results better than what you are currently experiencing. In certain cases, the baseline could take the form of a control group that runs concurrent with the group undergoing the intervention. Such a baseline would be helpful if you were attempting a new program with no past record with which to compare the outcomes.

A key consideration when planning any action research intervention is timing. How long should the experiment run? What would be a fair trial period in which to evaluate your intervention? Therefore, action research requires the development of a timeline. Unlike trial-and-error approaches in everyday practice, where one tries something for an indefinite period and usually does not specify a point at which to stop and see if things have actually changed, action research requires the establishment of a clear timeline. At a predetermined ending point, you stop and reflect on whether this approach is actually better than the old practice.

You also need to think about the proper criteria for evaluating your project. Whenever you try new interventions, you need to think about the best criteria for evaluation. What would be a successful outcome in this case? Unlike everyday practice, where investment of time and resources (and ego) often seem to justify continuing a practice even if the situation doesn't seem to be getting any better, action research requires that you reach a point of pause for informed reflection. At this point of reflection and assessment, you need to be able to decide whether you have met the criteria for success you set down in the planning stage, or whether you are on the road to meeting them. Obviously, not all new ideas or interventions will be successful at first. Some will have a measure of success, but will fall short of the level of effectiveness you were hoping to see.

When establishing the proper criteria for measuring the level of success from your intervention, a number of key questions will help in the process: How will the new approach be compared to the old approach?

On what basis will the results be evaluated at the project's end? What type of change will be deemed a success? How will action and change be observed and documented? How will you observe the project in a systematic way? With whom can you discuss this plan along the way and assess it at the conclusion?

We have found it useful in collecting data for action research to have the action researcher or the participants (or both) keep a reflective journal right from the beginning. You will tend to forget what you thought last week or observed yesterday in relationship to your action research project. A reflective journal is the one method we encourage all action researchers to use to help compensate for such memory lapses. Such a journal should always be part of the combination of methods employed to gain data.

It is also important to decide on several ways to collect data in action research. If you use multiple methods, the results of your action research will be more meaningful and hold greater validity for practice than if you use only a single method. The use of multiple methods in research is called triangulation.

Many methods of data collection are useful in action research. Figure 2.4 summarizes the major ones. Some of the standard ways to collect data in action research include noting and then comparing later results of *tests* of knowledge, for example, or number of days attended. *Records* like this are very useful. Develop a log to keep careful track of outcomes. Keeping a record and comparing how many times things happen can be a vital part of action research.

Interviews conducted by you or perhaps by another person—which often improves objectivity—can be invaluable. *Field notes*—ongoing notes on what you observe while an event is happening—can be a good source of data. Also, *anecdotal records* can be kept. This means jotting down incidents or anecdotes that may seem to have no pattern at the time but may reveal patterns later. *Audio recordings* or *videotaping* can also be invaluable.

Providing all the participants in your action research project with full knowledge about the project is important. In some cases, adult educators may find that their institutions require a signed document of consent from each participant before any action research project is initiated. Such informed consent signatures are required, for example, by most universities and colleges in compliance with federal regulations. You will need to ascertain how this approval should be obtained in your institutional setting.

Figure 2.4. Data-Gathering Techniques

Anecdotal records: Written, descriptive accounts of incidents. These may be accumulated until a broader picture or pattern emerges. Typically used to note a particular or repeating occurrence with a group or individual.

Field notes: Similar to anecdotal records, but the researcher's impressions and interpretations are recorded at the same time. Field notes may cover a broader range of observations than anecdotal records. They are typically written at the site of the event.

Document analysis: Documents typically include agency records, written reports, letters, memos, published materials at the locale, and learner reports or notes. These are particularly useful in trying to establish a baseline of what has happened in the past and can be invaluable for comparing a new approach to the past approach.

Logs: Typically, these are careful records of recurring activities that are often numerical. Examples include records of attendance, the number of times learners do certain things, or how groups allocate their time. Commentary in addition to the numerical entries can also be useful in building observed data.

Journals: Records of a person's reflections. These are typically written on a regular basis, for instance, at the end of the day or when there is relative calm. They allow one to express feelings, anxieties, and comments on events that have taken place or that one anticipates. This technique is particularly helpful in action research, because events and activities can change so much during a project that one can easily forget one's earlier thoughts and feelings. Looking back during the reflection stage is usually enriched by reflective journals kept by the researcher or the participants.

Portfolio: A collection of relevant materials compiled for a purpose. This is effectively a purposeful file of everything that may seem relevant to an issue. It may include learner papers, grades, relevant staff minutes, research articles, correspondence—any relevant item that should be kept for later review.

Questionnaires:
- *Open:* Ask for opinions or information in the participants' own words using open-ended questions. Especially useful for exploratory or subjective reactions, but can be difficult to analyze.
- *Closed:* These may require multiple-choice or direct short-answer responses. They seek specific information, with little room for the respondent's interpretations. Especially useful for collecting specific information.

Interviews: These allow for interaction and are usually considered superior to questionnaires when the issues may be emotionally charged or when participants may have difficulty with or even hostility toward a written instrument. Either the researcher or a third party can be the interviewer. The issue here is how the interviewer himself or herself may inhibit an open exchange with the participant. Interviews are often categorized into three types:

- *Structured:* Useful when seeking specific information on specific topics. This type leaves little room for discussion beyond the given questions. And if the interviewee begins to stray, the interviewer should bring him or her directly back to the questions.
- *Semi-structured:* Involves asking more open-ended questions of several participants but allows the interviewee to go further than the precise question with opinions, thoughts, and questions. Often written "probes" are used. These are reminders on the interview schedule of opening questions the interviewer can use to go to specific related aspects of the question after the opening response. For instance, the opening question might be, "How did you learn about this program?" After the general response, the interviewer could probe by asking if the participant had heard about it in the media or through word-of-mouth. The participant may mention other possibilities that the interviewer might not have mentioned or thought of.
- *Open:* Like the open questionnaire, this type encourages open discussion and wide-ranging opinion, with very little direction on the interviewer's part. Again, analysis of the collected data can be difficult, but the technique can open many areas the interviewer did not previously think of.

Audio and video recording: Valuable for getting an exact record of events, one that can reveal pauses, expressions, idioms, or body language. Since recording involves the use of mechanical devices, the person operating even a simple tape recorder needs to check and double-check the equipment beforehand. If it is to be used as part of an interview, the researcher needs to give careful thought to the interview questions beforehand.

Tests of learner performance: Objective or subjective tests of student achievement are the standard method of evaluating performance and diagnosing needs. These can be invaluable as pre- and posttests to help determine if change has occurred.

Let's return to our continuing example of the action research project in Allan's graduate class. As you may remember, the project was an in-class activity (a change in approach using mini-lectures), and written unanimous consent was gained from all of the students in advance. The first data-gathering technique chosen was a questionnaire to be used at the end of the project to help compare how the students felt about the old and new approaches to the readings. A second measure chosen was a midterm test, which compared scores on the current year's midterm with data from previous classes' midterms. Since it was possible that the new class was an unusual group, the comparison was based on the previous three years' midterm test results. The third measure chosen was a student reflective journal. Each student was asked to keep a journal with his or her reflections on the two methods and turn it in midway through the semester. Allan also kept a reflective journal, in which he noted observations after each class meeting, such as the comparative quality of the discussions in month one as opposed to month two. Finally, an in-class volunteer feedback committee of three students was established to give verbal feedback during and after the project. This committee provided a system for anonymous feedback from any of the students, who could talk with committee members during class breaks instead of talking directly to the instructor.

Here, then, were five methods of collecting data with which to triangulate and compare the old with the new intervention. Typically, the more methods for collecting and then cross-referencing data, the better the triangulation (Merriam, 1991). In general, we recommend at least three systems be involved, such as journals; test results, records, or logs; and questionnaires or interviews conducted by you or a third party.

Cycle One: Action Phase. The next phase in the action research cycle involves the action of the research, or the actual implementation of the intervention. This phase consists of the single step of implementing and observing. Let's examine this step in more detail.

Step Four: Implementing an Action and Observing the Results. Here is the actual doing—the action part of the research. This step requires good planning (the previous steps under the planning phase) and, done well, should be the most interesting phase of the research. Why? Because it feels so satisfying to at least try to do something better—to satisfy the "itch" that has driven the research process to this point. To successfully implement this crucial phase of the action research cycle, several questions must be answered: Am I staying true to the initial plan? Am I keeping close track of the data collection systems I have? Am I keeping in touch with my colleague, both to provide support for myself and to formulate ideas for what may be the next iteration of the project?

Cycle One: Reflection Phase. The final phase in the action research cycle is the reflection phase, which involves two steps. First, you must evaluate the actual outcomes of your intervention. Second, you must reflect on these outcomes and make decisions about future directions in light of the outcomes. Let's examine each of these steps.

Step Five: Evaluating the Results. When you have reached the end of the timeline in your action research project, it is important to dialogue with friends and colleagues and look together at the data collected. Action research requires that the adult education practitioner-researcher do more than merely offer a subjective determination that "things seem to be better or worse." Studying the gathered data is the last and most important step. Core questions at this point include the following: What do the data reveal about the problem and the intervention?

Were the criteria for success met? What do others think about the project? What are the tangible gains, if any? This is the point where evaluation is needed to determine just how successful the project has been thus far.

Let's again turn to our continuing example of an action research project. The data indicated that Allan's mini-lecture approach had helped improve the quality of discussion in his class. The students each indicated that they preferred this approach. The mean score of the midterm test was considerably higher compared to previous years. The feedback committee was unanimous in saying the project was a success. Beyond all of these measures, Allan had personally noted that the quality of the discussion had improved. Students were better prepared and more confident. More student thinking prior to discussion arose from the mini-lecture material, and new student insights from the readings began to emerge. Above all, Allan rarely heard that there was too much reading during the later classes using the mini-lecture format.

Step Six: Reflecting on the Project. After you have adequately evaluated the data from your project and provided some objective judgments about their relative worth, you are ready to move to the next step. Some core questions at this step include the following: Did the project produce promising results? Did the changes observed reflect what actually happened? How would this work better another time? If there is promise in this approach, should there be another cycle of action research? Asking such questions can lead to a much more fruitful result from action research. If your intervention has been successful, you must seriously consider conducting the same test or a variation on it again, because seeing the same results from repeated tests of the intervention increases the usefulness of the study. And it is worthwhile to ask if someone else can now try what you have found. Having your own finding repeated by others takes your findings to a higher level of usefulness. While you can't assume generalizability from your research, repeated like outcomes from an intervention increase the usefulness of your findings to others in similar settings of professional practice. Your descriptive accounts of action research projects can help others extrapolate to different cases and make a contribution to the knowledge base of your field.

Typically, the reflection stage is the weakest one for teachers, tutors, and administrators. Why? Often people are so busy in their jobs that they usually do not allow themselves time to reflect, to really look back. Perhaps feeling it is necessary to be active and productive rather than reflective is a phenomenon of our culture, but it is a serious shortcoming in regard to making professional gains in your own work or advancing your field overall. Others will want to know the results of your work, and they will want to try your interventions as well. Be assured that despite the feeling that what we do is somehow unique from what others do, there is more than enough in common among practitioners to make your outcomes of interest. Even if your project is only a partial success, or even if it is an outright failure, your colleagues will at least know that going in that direction seems less promising than going in another.

Let's conclude our example of the action research project in the graduate course. Allan felt this small project was a success. It definitely helped the students and changed the way he taught the course. But it was necessary to ask if it was a true test. Could the positive outcome have been due to the fact that the class under consideration happened to be made up of students who responded well to the mini-lecture? Did the students perhaps realize that Allan wanted them to do better during the mini-lecture stage and so worked harder out of respect for his wishes? To try to answer such questions, Allan decided to try the project again the next semester, this time with the mini-lecture in the first month, the old method in the second. The results were the same. Incidentally, Allan reported the results of this action research project at a meeting of adult education professors that fall, and asked others to try it. Two professors decided to try the method and found that students preferred the mini-lecture and performed better in similar introductory courses at their universities too, providing the ever-widening verification that increases the usefulness of the project.

The next obvious question was whether such an approach would work in senior courses—those beyond the introduction class. Allan tried the mini-lecture in two senior-level classes, but found that the mini-lectures were more successful with new (for example, newly returning adult) students than with senior ones. Apparently, since senior-level students usually organize themselves well, know how to read materials better than new students, and are more confident or more socialized to discussion-based classes, the senior students actually felt a bit patronized by the mini-lecture. The conclusion of the project was that this method works best with adults newly returning to graduate classes, whose academic organization skills are rusty. Remembering that the original students were convinced that the problem was too much reading, what do you think the action research revealed about their diagnosis of the problem and Allan's early diagnosis?

Possible Practitioner Questions for Action Research

What are the possibilities of action research for professional practice settings? Since so much of what we do in adult education is basically learning on the job, there is a tendency to place great value on what has already been done, which we discover through the advice and materials of others. Professional socialization processes also affect practitioners through a subtle pressure to "go with the flow" in the sense of either not trying new ideas or, if we do, undervaluing their significance. Both these realities—the pressures from professional socialization and the value placed on the experiences of others—provide a strong argument for the value of action research to our field. Action research provides a method for learning more effectively from the successes of others and provides better ways to test and share our own work. Our field can only become the richer for it.

A good example of the collective usefulness of action research for the field of adult education is seen in adult basic education (ABE). In recent years we have trained a number of adult literacy practitioners in Pennsylvania using action research as a professional development tool. Their experiences reflect the diversity of issues that can be addressed through action research. Some of these practitioners have investigated new methods for teaching science, math, and English content. In several projects, teachers have compared their new approaches with the methods they inherited from other adult teachers or from their own experiences as students. One ABE English teacher tested peer teaching of essay writing in English classes compared with her previous teacher-centered presentations. Another set up a project to find the most popular novels in her program and began to build a "reading tree" to instill more excitement about reading.

The majority of ABE practitioners studied ways to deal with retention. One action researcher compared the effect of a student support group in a literacy tutoring program with the common one-on-one model. Others have experimented to see if retention improves when there is a student "buddy system." Several have tested to see if increased counselor contact makes a difference in retention, and others have tried increased tutor-contact hours. Some have compared small literacy tutor groups with one-on-one tutoring. New ways to recruit students have been tried as well. A GED program at a correctional center has experimented with involving prison staff and guards in recruitment. Another person in a corrections setting managed to move the program to continuous intake instead of weekly intake.

Although the previous examples of research projects in ABE are useful, they most certainly do not exhaust the possibilities. Literacy practitioners have tried not only new methods and techniques, but also fundamental changes based on different teaching philosophies. One teacher had regularly been told that her learners had little to contribute to the planning and managing of ABE courses. Course syllabi were given out; no input was sought from learners. As a result, she had taken all the responsibility, and there was little ownership or involvement on the part of the learners once the course had begun. After trying a student planning committee for early input, she compared the collected journals, grades, and results from both her own observations and those of a fellow teacher against those of past courses. She found the project led to increased participation and higher grades in her ABE classes.

It would be most valuable for teachers and administrators to test the stereotypes we have inherited regarding low-literacy adults. For instance, what are the self-esteem levels of learners in and out of the classroom? What are the self-esteem levels given different types of learner ownership in courses? How does learner self-esteem change when classes have field trips, open discussions, or debates? If you are a literacy teacher who places vocational and job preparation above self-esteem issues as a program goal, why not compare the effects of some on-the-job observation or actual experience as opposed to no such job site experience? Why not test to see if vocational terminology learned in class makes a difference on the job? Does involvement of computers or other technology help recruit or retain students—especially males? Does use of computers help recruit or retain trainees on the job?

If you lean toward a liberal education and enrichment orientation for your learners, you might ask some of the following questions: Does the teaching of classic literature in high-interest/low-vocabulary books increase reading interest overall? What are the best books to use across common situations? What is the success level of students who develop their own materials? Can case studies of problem-solving techniques be used to test whether reading increases or critical thinking is enhanced?

Finally, if you are a literacy educator interested in learner empowerment, why not compare retention rates or cognitive gain around student action advocacy projects, such as working as a group to change a life problem? An example with which I have experience is a case where two African American learners felt that their landlord was discriminating against them. They were apparently receiving higher rent increases than other tenants. They organized a set of advocacy steps with their instructor and classmates to investigate this question. They raised both legal questions and constituent questions at the city council level. Their rent went back down. Would addressing such real-life problems increase retention? What is the impact of using real problems for teaching?

In the next chapter, six case studies of action research are presented to give practical examples of how the steps in the cycle of action research can be implemented to address actual practice problems and issues. These cases will flesh out the phases of planning, acting, and reflecting that tie together the action research process.

Conclusion: The Wider Value of Action Research

Adult education practitioners often find in our practice settings that we need to do more than just "do a good job." Pressures of evaluation and accountability force us to account for what we do. Such accountability may seem to be just one more thing in an all-consuming workload. The very number of things that must be done in a typical week in our jobs can seem to demand all of our energy and resources just to keep things moving as they are. Yet we must recognize that advances and improvements can arise from our accountability activities. We often want to make changes, try new approaches, and challenge old ideas, but we have no time. We often need new resources to make change possible, but there are no new resources. Or are there? Whether accounting for what we do, trying something new, or making a case for new resources, the matter often comes down to whether or not we have a strong case. And we often lack the evidence—the data—to show that resources can be allocated in better ways. As discussed in Chapter One, we often cannot show improved cost-effectiveness because we do not have the data and we lack the ways to gain evidence that new creative ways can make a difference. Anecdotes and statements of need are rarely good enough to justify serious change at the institutional or policy level. From local boards to the federal government, we need to be able to convince decision makers that we can make improvements. Research makes an enormous difference, and action research may be just the verified research we need.

As we have seen in this chapter, action research is hands-on research that every teacher or administrator can do. This approach empowers teachers, tutors, and administrators to take common problems in different parts of a state and try a similar approach, continually comparing action research outcomes along the way, continually sharing and ultimately developing a range of tested, replicated answers. A critical mass of data can suggest which new approaches are more promising than all the old ones. A case can be made to boards based on such regional or statewide data. And, internally, we can gain new ways to talk about common problems.

Action research provides the basic research tools to move ahead on common concerns. Action research widely shared offers the promise of real empowerment and professional development for long-term impact in our field of practice. The following appendix is an action research planner that you can use to guide your efforts in developing an action research project. Think through an issue or problem, discuss it with a friend, and begin today to develop new effectiveness in problem posing and problem solving within your practice as an adult educator.

Appendix: Developing Your Action Research Project

Planning Phase

Step One: Understanding the Problem
1. What actually is the problem? (Try to state in one sentence.)
2. Why do you think the problem exists? How do others see it?
3. Have studies been done on this issue? What have others said in the literature?
4. Is this a problem you want to spend time on, and will others agree to help you?
5. What are the most obvious reasons for or causes of the problem?
6. List any initial ideas you have on how to intervene.

Step Two: Defining the Project
1. How can you intervene with a new strategy or approach to see if it would make a difference? What can you do differently? How will you do it? Describe the proposed intervention in general terms.
2. When will you begin? Explain why.
3. Can you conduct this project in a way that allows you to manage and observe the activities? How will you manage the effects that will result?
4. What materials or equipment will you need? Explain why.
5. Whose approval is needed?
6. How will you inform the participants and gain their consent? How will you explain the project to the participants and what will you do if some do not want to participate?
7. Which colleagues would you like to discuss and evaluate your work? With whom can you discuss this plan along the way, and who will help to assess it at the conclusion?

Step Three: Determining the Measures
1. Specify the current or past baseline that will be used as a point of comparison. How will the new approach be compared to the old approach?
2. Specify the criteria for success. Describe the reasons for these criteria.
3. What is the timeline for the evaluation? For exactly how long should you run the project?
4. Specify the methods to be used to collect the data. How will action and change be observed and documented? How can you observe the project in a systematic way?
5. What might discourage you from finishing this project?

Action Phase

Step Four: Implementing an Action and Observing the Results
1. Are you staying true to the initial plan? Are you collecting the data the way you said you would? Are your data collection systems effective in helping you keep close track of what is going on?
2. Are you keeping in touch with your colleague, both for support in seeing the project through and to begin formulating ideas for what may be the next iteration of the project?
3. Provide a summary of the data collected.

Reflection Phase

Step Five: Evaluating the Results
1. What do the data reveal about your problem and the intervention?
2. Were your criteria for success met? How far were you from attaining them? What were the tangible gains, if any?
3. What do others think about the project?

Step Six: Reflecting on the Project
1. How could you repeat this intervention (or have it repeated) to develop more validity?
2. Will you enter a second cycle of the project? A third? If not, discuss why not.

References

Argyris, C. *Reasoning, Learning and Action: Individual and Organizational.* San Francisco: Jossey-Bass, 1982.

Cervero, R. M. *Effective Continuing Education for Professionals.* San Francisco: Jossey-Bass, 1988.

Houle, C. O. *Continuing Learning in the Professions.* San Francisco: Jossey-Bass, 1980.

Kemmis, S. and McTaggart, R. (eds.). *The Action Research Planner.* Geelong, Australia: Deakin University Press, 1984.

Mekosh-Rosenbaum, V. *Action Research Guide for Adult Literacy Practitioners.* Bethlehem, Pa.: Tri-Valley Literacy Staff Development, Lehigh University, n.d.

Merriam, S. B. *Case Study Research in Education: A Qualitative Approach.* San Francisco: Jossey-Bass, 1991.

Quigley, A. *Pennsylvania Action Research Handbook and Project Planner.* Harrisburg: Pennsylvania Department of Education, 1995.

Schön, D. *The Reflective Practitioner.* New York: Basic Books, 1983.

GARY W. KUHNE is assistant professor of adult education at Pennsylvania State University and an evaluator/trainer in the Pennsylvania Action Research Network.

B. ALLAN QUIGLEY is associate professor and regional director of adult education at Pennsylvania State University and director of the Pennsylvania Action Research Network.

This chapter presents six case studies of action research projects in various adult education settings: a museum, a church, a prison, a homeless shelter, a university, and a hospital.

Case Studies of Action Research in Various Adult Education Settings

Gary W. Kuhne, Drucie Weirauch, David J. Fetterman, Raiana M. Mearns, Kathy Kalinosky, Kathleen A. Cegles, Linda Ritchey

Introduction

Gary W. Kuhne

This chapter examines six case studies of action research in a variety of adult education settings, including problems within the context of museum education, adult religious education, corrections education, higher education, adult basic education, and continuing professional education. Why, you might ask, are case studies important, when it has already been stated elsewhere in this sourcebook that action research findings are not generalizable? McTaggart (1991, p. 168) provides the best answer: "When trying to decide on concrete action in a particular situation, it helps to know how others fared in similar or related circumstances. In this respect, descriptive accounts of concrete cases can be useful to make extrapolations to different cases." Although action research findings may not be generalizable in the classical sense of research generalizability, one can definitely extrapolate from such studies to other situations. Such extrapolations are highly useful in critical reflection on findings from other practice settings.

In this chapter we will see six case studies of action research projects. Each of the six practitioner-researchers had participated in an informal course on action research with Allan Quigley and began formulating his or her question with the problem-posing assistance of the class members. Later—for some, months later—each implemented the process of action research in a

NEW DIRECTIONS FOR ADULT AND CONTINUING EDUCATION, no. 73, Spring 1997 © Jossey-Bass Publishers work-related problem. The format for each case is based on the steps for action research projects in Chapter Two. Let's turn our attention to these cases.

Action Research and Faculty Development in a Museum

Drucie Weirauch

I work as a program specialist for a large museum, where educational programs are based on art, science, music, and literature. There are separate program specialists for adult art classes and adult natural history classes. I am responsible for recruiting instructors and for developing, administering, and evaluating courses for adults in music and literature.

Ask a museum curator, and he or she will tell you that a museum is a collection of objects. Exhibitions are carefully designed to be attractive and to convey information. Less attention is paid to the viewer than to the viewed. Formal museum education, likewise, tends to be object-based, whether it is a course on Egyptology, a docent-led tour of French Impressionism, or in my case, for example, a course on the American short story or listening to chamber music.

Understanding the Problem. When I started to work at the museum, I inherited a number of instructors who had taught classes for several years. Many taught at area universities and used the same subject-centered, lecture-dominated methods with the adults that they used with undergraduates. The instructors came to class with prepared syllabi and daily lesson plans, stubbornly adhering to the subject. They rarely took the time to find out about the adults' expectations for the class or their abilities and prior knowledge of the subject. Furthermore, the instructors taught using traditional methods and techniques. Reading from copious notes, augmented by occasional overhead transparencies or notes on the blackboard, was the norm. In short, the classes were prescribed, inflexible, and boring to a number of the adult students, who in some cases knew a great deal about the subject. The problem, therefore, leading to my action research project was the fact that some instructors tend to use mostly subject-centered, teacher-directed approaches, dominated by lecture or demonstration, with little concern or appreciation for their adult students' needs, abilities, or experiences.

Defining the Project. With a clear picture of the problem, I then turned attention to deciding what strategies I could use to help the instructors shift their focus from the subject to the learner and make them aware of the importance of the adult learners' experiences and expectations. The hoped-for benefits of such strategies included better instruction, more meaningful classes, and higher student satisfaction, which ultimately meant better attendance and recurring registrations for future classes.

It was clear that the proposed intervention had to be different from earlier attempts at professional instructional development, since "lecture teachers" had already shown they were reluctant to change. They regarded their subjects as academic and wanted to preserve their academic/expert pedagogical stance. Twice before, I had attempted to redirect the instructors' approach, first with a two-hour "Teaching the Adult Learner" workshop and second, after observing their classes, by offering suggestions on how to attend to adult learners' expectations and needs. Neither was successful. Moreover, it was uncomfortable for me to pose as the expert and tell them what to do, which was precisely what I was trying to change in their teaching behavior. To help the instructors see the importance of learners' needs and experiences, it was important that I not hypocritically posture as the expert; the teachers must be involved in the process.

Evaluation is predicated on expectation. It measures how we expect a person to behave, what we expect them to know or do. It had been my experience that while instructors wanted to know what was expected, they did not want to be told what to do. I decided that my intervention would be to revise the evaluation procedure to reflect my expectations for learner-centered teaching. Evaluation is especially effective when the person being evaluated helps to set the expectations. However, the evaluation form historically used in adult museum classes was a standard Likert-scale questionnaire, a "happygram" of student satisfaction with the course, the teaching, the facility. Like most evaluations of this kind, it rendered little helpful information and did little to improve practice. My intervention, revising the evaluation form, was selected to reflect the expectations of learner-centered teaching. At the start of the course, both instructors and students would list their goals for the class on the form. This would engage the instructors in the process of setting expectations for their class and allow the students to indicate their personal goals and experience.

The time frame involved was more than a full semester, or about twelve weeks. I contacted the instructors three weeks before courses were to begin to explain the action plan and anticipated results. I had to give them time to write their goals for the course and revise them for the form. The evaluation form was used at the first class and again on the last day of class. Because some courses lasted only one day and others up to eight weeks, the time between evaluations varied for each course. One day per class was required to compile the responses and have a follow-up discussion with the instructor.

The director of my department gave approval for revising the form and to trying the intervention. Approval was also obtained from all of the instructors. I sent them a letter describing the revised form and its intended use for professional instructional development. I explained how it would give them better information about students' abilities in relation to the instructor's goals for the class and also provide individuals' expectations and goals. I also explained that by providing the methods, techniques, and materials for the form, they would later be able to learn what was effective. I invited the instructors to call me for clarification; several did. Finally, I explained that the evaluation was formative, that they could read the results first and keep the forms for up to two weeks. I wanted the forms back ultimately so that I could review the results and then talk to the instructors about the evaluation. No one else would see the results, and each instructor's results would be confidential. When I started my action research, I had an intern for the semester. A graduate student in adult education, she was aware of effective ways to teach adults and could provide an extra set of eyes for monitoring the project. In addition, I shared the general research results with my director, always keeping the instructors' identities confidential.

Determining the Measures. The baseline for comparison was past observations and evaluations of the instructors. Criteria for success included improved student satisfaction as indicated on the revised evaluation form and satisfaction voiced by the instructors themselves. It is best to have multiple perspectives when monitoring an action research intervention. This plan called for responses from me, another observer, the instructor, and the students. I kept a journal from the inception of the project planning to the end. In it I recorded the reactions of the instructors to the initial request, their concerns and attitudes, and the goals they supplied. I also recorded my own ideas and concerns. Observation provided more data. During observation, I recorded the classroom climate, the methods and techniques in use, the exchange of ideas, the number of times students provided information, and how the instructor responded to questions. My graduate intern did the same. The evaluation form itself provided documentation on the students' needs, how and if they were fulfilled, and their personal goals. Additionally, the students indicated their satisfaction with the chosen methods, techniques, and materials in both Likert-scale items and open-ended questions. Finally, a postcourse interview with the instructors provided me with information on how successful the revised form and the instructors' involvement in the evaluation process were in helping them better understand their teaching.

A number of possible constraints were obvious. Time, as always, was a consideration. The intervention could not take too much of my time; moreover, it could not impose excessive demands on the instructors or they would resist. Another possible constraint was instructor resistance to the idea in general. The instructors, especially veteran ones, did not want to be told how to teach. This intervention was time-efficient for both me and the instructors, and it was nonthreatening. For uniformity and overall program improvement, all instructors were asked to participate, not just the subject-centered ones. The results of the observation and the evaluation were confidential, to reduce any perceived threat to future teaching opportunities. Finally, it was possible that the students would not assess themselves or provide additional goals, thereby providing no information to the instructor. I hoped to avoid this by keeping the form simple.

Implementing an Action and Observing the Results. Three weeks before classes began, instructors were sent a form asking them to indicate five to eight course goals, as well as methods, techniques, and materials. When I received them, I integrated them with a base evaluation form, which took only about ten minutes per course. The goals were on page one. There was space at the bottom of that page for students to indicate personal goals and expectations. Methods and materials were integrated in Likert-scale questions on page two. On the first night of class, students were given the evaluation form and asked to complete page one only. They assessed their own knowledge and skills in comparison with the instructor-provided goals using a "high," "medium," "low," or "don't know" response. At the bottom of the page they wrote their personal expectations or goals for the class. Students were told they could remain anonymous if they so chose but should mark their evaluation form in some way so that they could retrieve it at the end of the course. The instructors collected the forms and read them in order to learn about their students, then gave them to me. In some courses, those where I especially felt there was some resistance, I attended the first night as an official museum administrator to explain the purpose of the form and oversee the first stage.

After I received the evaluation forms I called the instructor to discuss the student self-assessments and goals and to ascertain how the instructor planned to attend to these. I observed each class at least once during the semester to see how things were going and to record my observations. In some cases I was able to compare observations with past classes. During my observation I noted interactive methods, student-centeredness, teacher-dominance, and what was being covered. On the last day I returned the evaluation forms to the instructors to redistribute to the class. After the students completed the forms, the instructors collected and reviewed them, then gave them to me.

Evaluating the Results and Reflecting on the Project. The brief, casual consultation with the instructors after the first night of class proved to be interesting and encouraging. The students' personal goals revealed to the instructor the diversity in motivation and abilities in the classroom. With these concrete, written comments, we were able to marvel at the students' diversity, share ideas, and discuss strategies. There was no typical student. Examples of the range of interest and experience include the following:

Storytelling. A businesswoman wrote that she wanted to integrate storytelling with her business presentations to liven them up. A Sunday School teacher wanted to be better at telling Bible stories. A grandmother was working on her oral history as a legacy for her grandchildren.

How to write a cookbook. This class in particular had students with different needs. One participant had already written and published a cookbook. She became a valuable resource. Many just wanted to collect family recipes and present them to family members. Others were fundraising for their school or church. Still another woman was hoping for an advance from a major publisher for her cookbook on African cooking. An ESL student, she had ambitious goals, but limited language skills.

Theatrical make-up. One student worked in a rehabilitation hospital. She wanted to learn about make-up to help her patients conceal deformities from burns and accidents. Others were merely preparing for Halloween.

Journal making. This class had students of all levels, from those just beginning to keep a journal to those who had used lifelong journal entries to create fiction. Several had had short stories published. In fact, one student had published a successful book.

Diary of a small business owner. The first page of the evaluation gave students a forum in which to express their experience and their expectations and offered the instructors valuable information about individual needs.

My observation of each class documented increases in learner-centered teaching and in meeting the needs and experience level of the students. Likewise, my graduate intern reported that there was ample evidence of andragogical methods (Knowles, 1980) in the classes. In all cases I received the completed forms from the instructors. Sometimes, however, students did not complete the entire form or neglected to complete it at all. This was disappointing, but not surprising. The results from the revised evaluation forms were positive and exciting for both me and the instructors. In many cases the students' self-assessment at the beginning of the class was "low" or "don't know." By the end of the class, they were rating themselves "high." This was encouraging to the instructor and much more valuable than a simple "good" rating on general instruction. Furthermore, because goals were specified, the instructor could determine specifically where he or she was strong or weak. What was particularly interesting was how many students annotated their Likert-scale responses with comments like "I feel I cannot give myself a 'high,' simply because I think I can get better at writing poetry. But [the instructor] helped me see how to get started and how to move on. She motivated me more than I thought possible. I will continue to write, and maybe someday I'll feel I merit a 'high.'"

I interviewed the instructors after their courses were over, by phone. My interviews, therefore, were casual and individualized. I made a point of talking about the students' diversity in ability and needs. I commented on my observations and the comments I received from my intern. In all cases we discussed the responses to the open-ended questions on the evaluation form. Fortunately, the project was successful, and I did not have to share many concerns or negative evaluation results. However, in a few cases, students indicated that a certain technique did not work very well or that handouts, for example, were poor. Though negative, these remarks were still valuable, and changing the technique or handout was easy. The instructors felt this new form provided them with valuable information about their students and their teaching. Because the form required little of their time yet yielded positive results, they embraced this system. I have used it now for two years, with continued success.

Action Research and Increased Participation in a Church

David J. Fetterman

I am a United Methodist minister in charge of religious education at a large suburban church. The adults in the congregation are of all ages; however, there is a large group in the 35–50 age range who have children or youths living in their homes. According to the 1990 census, the community at large exhibits the same demographic characteristics as the church membership.

Understanding the Problem. After examination of our congregation's religious education attendance records, it was discovered that our adult religious education reaches basically the same audience regardless of the program; the people are just recycled from program to program. It was also determined that there was a large group of nonparticipating adults in the baby boomer age range (that is, born between 1946 and 1964) who could be considered "resident members." Resident members were defined by isolating those who lived in the same zip code as the church building, as well as in the zip codes of contiguous communities.

We definitely had a recruitment and participation problem in the church adult education programs. Given the low level of participation in the church adult education programs and the community and congregational demographics, the problem question to be used in our action research design was, could we increase adult participation in religious education through innovative programming?

Defining the Project. The group that provides oversight for religious education ministries in our congregation is the education commission. That commission considered the findings from the problem step. They adopted the proposed plan of action, which called for them to recruit an adult task force that would have as inclusive a membership as possible (in terms of participating and nonparticipating adults, gender, age, and so forth). Task force responsibilities would include examining and evaluating our current adult religious education offerings; assessing the needs of the nonparticipating baby boomer target population; developing plans for religious education programming targeted at this group; and recommending action plans to the education commission for prioritization and implementation.

Members of the education commission contacted potential task force members to solicit their participation. Each recruiter had a copy of the action research proposal that had been previously adopted. Problems could have arisen later if different recruiters had told potential members different things. To maximize effectiveness, all members had to be given the same information. Two of the members were asked to serve as co-conveners for the group.

When the task forces were finalized, we all met for lunch. At the luncheon, the commission chairperson and I distributed to each task force member copies of their responsibilities, then made an oral presentation to help delineate those responsibilities. Then we gave an opportunity for discussion in the whole group to ensure that members were confident in their understanding of their job. Finally we sent them to another room to conduct their first meeting. Subsequent meetings were scheduled by the group at their convenience.

By design, the chairperson and I did not attend any meetings beyond the first one. Because we were authority figures, if we had attended, members might have deferred to us for opinions and approval, which would have prevented free dialogue. Also, if we were defined as parts of the problem, our presence would have inhibited honest sharing of that perception. Instead of attending meetings, we established several dates by which we wanted progress reports, as well as a final date for the project. These benchmarks were designed to provide accountability and movement in the process while maximizing honest sharing.

To prevent the project from dragging on endlessly, the task force needed a timeline. The education commission established the following schedule:

March 14	Education commission defines the problem.
March 14–April 16	Adult task force is recruited.
April 23–June 30	Adult task force conducts it work.
July 1–September 30	Task force report is submitted to the commission, which then develops plans for implementation.
September 30– November 30	Specific plans are developed for the adult forum.
December 1–31	Marketing of the adult forum.
January 14– February 18	Adult forum meets; an evaluation is conducted.
March 13	Education commission reflects on evaluations and prepares for Cycle 2.

Determining the Measures. The task force determined that the church needed to offer short-term courses that did not require attendance at every session. Such courses needed to be beneficial, with topics that were specific and had direct, immediate applications for participants. New program efforts, therefore, needed to be short-term, with freestanding sessions united by an umbrella theme of direct, practical benefit to participants. These findings led to several recommendations. One proposal that was adopted for immediate testing was the concept of an adult forum: a series of short-term classes with umbrella themes but freestanding sessions.

The topic for the initial adult forum was selected from a list provided by the adult task force. This program was to complement, not replace or compete with, existing adult programming. A measure of success was established: participation by five to ten currently nonparticipating adults. The methods of data collection and evaluation were adopted and included a survey questionnaire of participants, informal interviews with participants, and comparison of prior attendance records and those for this forum.

Implementing an Action and Observing the Results. The adult forum was conducted as a seminar, with participants seated around tables. There was no textbook; instead, discussion would occur based on a video series. The education commission chairperson and I were cofacilitators for the series but did not present ourselves as content experts. Our role was to lead discussion, not lecture. The atmosphere was informal. Incorporating the needs and experiences of participants was integral to the forum. Coffee and tea were provided.

Evaluating the Results and Reflecting on the Project. Results from the three evaluative tools were as follows: The comments from the informal interviews were very positive, with participants citing the program content (the video series) as a big draw, and most saw the group interaction in an informal environment as valuable. The surveys were also very positive. On reflection, we needed to decide whether the forum's success was related to the format chosen, the famous person associated with the video used, or both. The attendance records showed a range of five to eleven formerly nonparticipating adults in the forum, thus meeting the criterion for success.

Several issues from the evaluation data that we consider consider performing a second cycle of action research. The question of why the forum was successful (the format, the person associated with the video, or some combination of the two) needs to be investigated in a further adult forum. We also determined that there needs to be additional time for discussion and interaction in future adult forums so we can better assess this component. Although the need for additional discussion time did not appear as an issue in the original three evaluative tools, it was observed in the diaries of the facilitators as a need. Finally, we need to investigate using a nontraditional time slot, as well as this nontraditional format, in future forums. We decided to use only a nontraditional format in the first attempt, believing that it would be difficult to assess the variables of format and time simultaneously. Having used the nontraditional format in a traditional time slot, we can examine the nontraditional time slot in future cycles of action research.

Action Research and Retaining Literacy Volunteers in a Corrections Center

Raiana M. Mearns

I was coordinator of a countywide literacy program in a relatively rural area. It was my responsibility to recruit volunteer tutors to work with low-level readers. Each year we were able to train thirty to forty volunteers from the community to tutor basic reading or English as a second language. My action research project focused on a problem involving the literacy program at our county prison. This literacy effort was chronically understaffed because it takes a special person to want to work in this environment.

Understanding the Problem. After contending for some time with the staffing problems in the prison, I was pleased and surprised when students from a private liberal arts college showed an interest in volunteering for this program. Wanting to act on such unanticipated interest, I advertised a twelve-hour training program in tutoring basic reading, using flyers, newspaper advertisements, and e-mail. Once we recruited some college students for the class, we provided an orientation and visitation at the actual prison. We ended up with ten trained volunteer college tutors willing to work at the prison. These students were assigned to work alongside a VISTA (Volunteers in Service to

America) volunteer and several community volunteer tutors. We had used some college tutors in the past, but this time we concentrated our efforts to decide how we could best use these volunteers.

Now that we had the tutors, we needed to find inmates willing to get involved in the literacy effort. Approximately fifteen male inmates volunteered to participate in the program, less than ten percent of the total prison population. The female inmates were involved in a separate program run by two college students as a graded project for their English class and thus were not a part of this research project. The inmates requested various types of instruction, ranging from GED preparation to study of classical literature. One-on-one instruction was used as much as possible, in order to individualize each student's learning experience. The college tutors added a spark of youthful enthusiasm that was not present in our group of primarily retired community volunteers.

A drawback of working in a corrections facility is that the population is in constant flux. Inmates are often transferred or denied privileges without notice. In addition, the mood of a prison student was often very irregular, depending on circumstances beyond our control. Volunteer tutors can become discouraged when their students are not motivated or consistent in attendance. On the other hand, college students often have very busy schedules and must work tutoring time in between other activities.

All of these factors contributed to a problem with tutor retention, which I saw as the proper focus for my action research project. I didn't want to lose the college tutors, but adjusting to their schedules was often frustrating and resulted in a lack of cohesiveness in the program. The students of community tutors were asked to double up with students of college tutors when the college tutors did not show.

Defining the Project. A potential intervention to address the tutor retention problem came through the financial aid office at the college. They wanted to know if we would be willing to employ a college student part-time during the school year at a minimal cost to the council. As I considered this potential position, I began to see how such a person could have a positive impact on the college tutor retention problem. Specifically, the intervention for the action research project was to try using a college student as coordinator of tutoring to increase retention of college tutors. I knew that it would decrease the time I spent playing telephone tag, but I wasn't sure how students would react to another student being in charge. Using action research, I was able to find the answer to this question.

Determining the Measures. I hoped this intervention would create a number of benefits. Certainly increased retention of college tutors was a desired outcome, which in turn could help to maintain a good relationship with the college. I also hoped for less time spent by staff on scheduling, as well as continuity of instruction for the prison inmates. Perhaps most of all, I hoped to see less dependence on community tutors to fill in for unavailable college tutors.

I decided that retention of 60 percent of college tutors would indicate success for this plan. The previous year only 30 percent of the college tutors had stayed until the end of the school year. I decided to run the prison tutoring program from September through May. Informal tutoring could continue through the summer if desired. All tutors met with students on Monday nights from 7:00 to 9:00.

I needed to do a number of things to implement this action research strategy. First, I needed to obtain approval from the prison board and the literacy council advisory board. Next, I needed to hire and train the student coordinator, introduce the coordinator to all prison tutors, and make a plan for scheduling. I required the student coordinator to keep attendance records and a journal. Another person, the overall coordinator, would also observe tutoring sessions periodically.

To collect data for the action research project, I decided to survey both the tutors and the inmates to determine satisfaction with the program. I also interviewed with the warden and deputy warden to determine their satisfaction with the program. I next decided that I needed to read the coordinator's journal and reflect on the findings. Finally, I decided that I would evaluate the attendance records to see if my success criterion was met (60 percent retention of college tutors).

Implementing an Action and Observing the Results. As the project progressed, I discovered that both the college tutors and the community tutors indicated an increased satisfaction with the program. The student coordinator proved very successful in scheduling tutoring sessions to everyone's satisfaction. The only difficult period was over Christmas break. Inmates overwhelmingly stated that time spent on tutoring was worthwhile. They requested that additional time be allotted for tutoring. Retention of tutors was not as high as I had hoped. Attendance records indicated a 50 percent retention over the school year. The major reason given for discontinuing tutoring was still scheduling conflicts at the college.

Evaluating the Results and Reflecting on the Project. The student coordinator was a good solution for me, because coordination of tutoring took less of my time than prior to the project. The growing problem with community tutors feeling taken advantage of when college tutors didn't show up for scheduled tutoring sessions was successfully resolved. The college students who chose to tutor did not feel they were harassed into volunteering their time. The college felt their students were contributing positively to the surrounding community. By submitting this plan to the regional staff development office, I was able to obtain an action research grant of $300 that paid the student coordinator's salary. Most important, the prison inmates benefited by having enthusiastic tutors visit them weekly to help them achieve their educational goals.

On reflection, I saw several problems with retention still remaining. Potential college student tutors will always be faced with a busy schedule that will conflict with tutoring. While a student coordinator can't change this reality of college life, retention was positively affected, even if not to the level I had hoped. Overall, I thought that the benefits outweighed the drawbacks. The prison population is a difficult one to work with, and we needed as many interested tutors as we could train. Some of the students were more interested in the training and how it would look on their résumé, but for the most part the students were refreshing and helpful to their prison students. I enjoyed their energy, but in the long run, the most faithful tutors were those from the community. The council was very fortunate to have such committed community support.

Action Research and Learner Participation in a Homeless Shelter

Kathy Kalinosky

I am a literacy teacher at a long-term homeless shelter for women in a small town on the outskirts of a metropolitan city. The shelter is a large facility formerly used as a convent. The long-term residents each have their own bedroom, but share all other common areas. Each resident must also prepare her own meals. As I sought to help the long-term residents increase their reading skills, I encountered a problem that action research seemed to offer hope of solving.

Understanding the Problem. As I began to provide instruction at this site, I was surprised to discover that many of the shelter residents were reluctant to come out of their rooms to attend the literacy classes I was hired to teach. I used action research to explore various ideas on how to engage this recalcitrant group.

I first identified the problem in the form of a researchable question, "How can I motivate homeless shelter residents to attend 'Getting Active' sessions? Getting Active sessions focused on life-skill building and served as a bridge to further literacy, ABE, and GED sessions by breaking down social barriers to participation. The most obvious reasons for lack of attendance seemed to be that residents didn't know when sessions were held or what was being covered, or they weren't interested in participating. Since twenty-one women were currently residing at the shelter and only three or four residents were attending each session, I hoped this project would result in an increase in enrollment and attendance of shelter residents at the Getting Active sessions.

Defining the Project. I met with the center director to discuss the difficulties I was facing and obtained her recommendations on how to increase attendance. I obtained the necessary approvals from the center director and my program director to conduct the action research project. The shelter residents who attended the previous sessions were informed of the project and agreed to participate because they wanted to see more residents involved in the program. They hoped such involvement would improve both attitudes and living conditions in the shelter. From the beginning, an initial group of participants took ownership of the problem and assisted in finding a solution.

Part of the power of action research is that participants can assist in arriving at the solution, so I established an advisory committee consisting of the individuals who were already attending. I also enlisted the assistance of my program coordinator and the regional staff development center director as colleagues with whom to discuss and evaluate my work.

Determining the Measures. I established the project baseline by reviewing attendance records of previous sessions, determining that the baseline was three to four individuals per session. The criterion for success was set at seven to eight individuals. If I could attract seven or eight individuals per session, I would consider the intervention used in that session successful in improving attendance in this setting. I decided that a realistic time for completing the project was two to four months, giving me ample time to gather enough data to determine which interventions were successful and met my criterion for success.

The advisory committee and I developed the following list of possible interventions to get residents to participate in the Getting Active sessions:

- Hold a lunch or dinner with testimony from a client at another shelter who had been involved in a similar program
- Conduct one-to-one interviews with shelter residents
- Have residents already attending bring another resident to a session
- Produce a newsletter for residents
- Supply information about sessions to other support agencies
- Print and post a schedule of events.

After consulting both the center's administrative staff and the program participants, we decided that a simple day or time change would not make a difference in attendance. In fact, if we changed the day or time, several of those attending would no longer do so.

Implementing an Action and Observing the Results. The action phase involved implementation of the project and collection of data through observation. The advisory committee and I decided that the first intervention would be a cooking activity, since we had already seen some positive results from this kind of activity. We planned a shelter dinner (which would be prepared by willing residents) in order to increase the program's visibility to other residents and give me the opportunity to speak with those attending. We listed the materials and equipment needed, developed the menu, formulated the shopping list, and decided on quantities needed to serve twenty people. Participants decided to provide their own ingredients for the smaller cooking projects of their favorite dishes, and action research money was used to purchase all other items for the menu, which included several salads, spare ribs, shrimp, french fries, corn on the cob, asparagus, carrots, pasta, Italian bread, frozen yogurt and ice cream with toppings.

Dinner was delicious and produced a turnout of nine residents. During and after dinner a discussion on the purpose of the literacy program was held. Residents shared ideas on how to recruit more people to the Getting Active sessions as the first step toward literacy training. Overall, it was a very successful experience, and we met our criterion for success. We implemented two more cooking sessions that weren't nearly as extravagant and also met our criterion for success.

Evaluating the Results and Reflecting on the Project. The reflection phase allowed us to evaluate the significance of the results and decide whether to enter another cycle of the project. The committee was pleased that more people showed up for cooking sessions and that we met our criterion for success; however, they wanted to see attendance continue to increase. They decided we should implement additional cycles of the action research project.

Additional Cycles of Action Research. In the second cycle of our action research project, the committee decided to produce a newsletter in order to create greater awareness of the literacy program among those who did not attend the dinner. The committee believed all residents were capable of reading the newsletter, so it was produced, reviewed, approved, and distributed by the committee, but no marked improvement in attendance or enrollment resulted.

In the third cycle, one-to-one interviews with residents were conducted by the adult literacy program counselor. Participants were not comfortable talking with the counselor, as they felt she was going to "psychoanalyze" them. In addition, only four residents participated in the interviews. General observations showed this to be an ineffective way to increase attendance.

The fourth and final cycle was instituted by the shelter administrative staff, who demanded a drastic change in the program content, requesting that I focus on job search workshops and change the format to highly structured formalized instruction resulting in a certificate of completion. Residents could earn a gift certificate for dinner at a local restaurant after receiving a certain number of certificates. This cycle was produced very poor results; participation dropped drastically, with no more than two residents attending any session. I have concluded that the homeless shelter residents resisted highly structured educational situations.

Further Reflection. From my observations and the counselor's one-to-one interviews, it is evident that clients in the homeless shelter are extremely uncomfortable interacting with others, particularly those with whom they share common areas in the shelter. They have difficulty effectively socializing with others or acting appropriately as a member of a group. However, based on data gathered through attendance records, enrollment records, journal entries, and informal interviews, I concluded that homeless shelter residents responded positively to cooking activities, meeting my goal of seven to eight participants.

I observed that homeless shelter residents need a very comfortable, easygoing atmosphere in which to test their abilities to interact with others. The cooking activities were held in the kitchen. Kitchens, in general, seem to be comfortable gathering and conversing places. During cooking activities, residents were able to participate without bringing direct attention to themselves. The primary focus was on the cooking activity; conversation and group dynamics were secondary. Participants had positive, nonthreatening opportunities to exercise socialization skills, and through instructor facilitation and role modeling, they were able to find alternatives to their ineffective interactive behaviors.

The research shows cooking activities led by the residents but facilitated by the instructor were very successful in motivating the homeless shelter residents to attend Getting Active sessions. The hidden bonus was the growth opportunity for residents to develop positive interaction skills. During cooking activities I observed that residents' attitudes and behaviors improved in the following areas: cooperation, problem solving, enjoyment, gratitude, pride, initiative, leadership, delegation, organization, communication, unsolicited interaction, and bonding.

This project was not without difficulties. The discouraging factors I encountered included an unsupportive shelter managerial staff that was inconsistent in disseminating information to me and to shelter residents, causing much dissension and disappointment. The administration in the homeless shelter did not provide strong support for residents, and this inconsistency caused an extremely high frustration level, contributing to residents' belief that they were not capable of independence and that nothing in life is fair. This eliminated any reason for residents to look for solutions or opportunities to learn the skills necessary to gain independence. They felt powerless to implement changes, and this powerlessness discouraged them from even trying to solve their problems.

Residents' lack of communication skills, self-respect, and self-confidence presented additional difficulties. This population exhibited a variety of feelings and emotions I did not anticipate, including fear, anger, resentment, guilt, shame, distrust, and paranoia. I found that their fears and inability to function in a group contributed greatly to their lack of attendance. I proceeded, however, to push on to obtain results and improve their attitudes and living circumstances. They are a tough crowd, but they are reachable, as evidenced by the fact that this project brought about obvious positive change, at least in the short term. Unfortunately, our program at the shelter soon ended.

Action Research and Technology Innovation in a University

Kathleen A. Cegles

I am a physical therapist educator at a private university in a northeastern city. A recurring problem in our department was recruiting qualified instructors to our smaller metropolitan university to teach in specialized content areas. Reflecting on this problem, it occurred to me that the use of an interactive teleconferencing link might hold promise for a solution. By establishing such a link with a qualified, experienced content expert from a larger university located two hundred miles away, our graduate student physical therapists would have access to course possibilities we would otherwise be unable to offer. This possibility provided the stimulus for an action research project.

Understanding the Problem. One course that seemed to offer a good possibility for such an interactive teleconferencing effort was a two-semester research course, a prerequisite for graduation that needed to be offered annually. When offered with an on-site instructor, the course included lecture, self-directed learning via workbook and computer statistics, along with traditional components of quantitative research: problem identification and hypothesis, literature review, data collection, and data analysis. A teleconferencing link with the off-site instructor could be organized in the following manner: The instructor would broadcast from his home campus classroom (remote site) via satellite to our students at a local elementary school (base site).

As I began to discuss this possibility further, I discovered a significant number of concerns expressed by some program faculty, university administrators, and technological support service personnel. These concerns included such things as logistical aspects and student acceptance. Of greater concern were issues related to contract negotiations among our university (base site), the broadcast university (remote site), and the local school district. Financial considerations also included accurately predicting the technology fees so that we could accurately project the total cost of the program initiative. Even the need for students to go to an off-campus classroom to receive the teleconferencing elicited some concern from our students and program director.

Defining the Project. It became clear in the face of such objections and concerns that a pilot project on a much smaller scale would be necessary to demonstrate the potential of teleconferencing to the university. I wanted to implement such a pilot (paper) project prior to full course development and troubleshoot any problems (real or perceived) that might arise. Action research seemed ideally suited to this project.

When it was obvious that the search for a qualified faculty member to teach this course would not be successful in sufficient time for delivery at the appropriate time in the curriculum, I discussed with the dean the possibility of searching for someone who would be willing to deliver the course via interactive teleconferencing. I was aware that our university already had the fiber-optic wiring in place (which represented the greatest required outlay for start-up costs) and some identified faculty, computer support staff, and select administrators who supported the concept of bringing distance education to our university. I therefore decided to proceed by investigating the distance education options available to me. No prior courses had been brought to our university by satellite delivery, but I knew that some satellite videoconference programming had been delivered to faculty as one-to two-hour speaker presentations.

I began to inquire around campus about persons who were interested in seeing distance education brought to our university and who would be willing to assist me in the implementation phase of this endeavor. I proceeded to meet with persons who I had identified as instrumental to the process: staff in computing and telecommunication's academic services division, the president of the university, and other program directors and faculty who I believed had the same vision. Each of the persons I contacted were interested in assisting with the project. I took the approach in my discussions that distance education was not something new and out of the ordinary, but was an adjunctive educational delivery method that would demonstrate the university's commitment to innovative educational programming and delivery in addition to fulfilling the need for a particular program's instructional course. I knew that to be successful, I needed the support of all the persons cited earlier.

In my discussions with key personnel on campus, I found that we had all the fiber-optic wiring required, but did not have the appropriate equipment to conduct an entire course over two semesters. I also found that our university belonged to a nonprofit consortium open to independent and community colleges, government agencies providing learning support services for K–12 institutions, and business and industry for the purpose of establishing a statewide videoconferencing and data network in which member institutions would create partnerships to share intellectual and administrative resources. I then secured the commitment of the university president to proceed with this action research project.

I was told at the time of my investigative process that two months before the start of the required course, the university would have the appropriate telecommunications equipment ready to operate in a dedicated technologically equipped classroom with tiered seating. I knew I had to move quickly over the next eight months to assure that all necessary equipment was secured, contracts completed, and a willing, qualified instructor identified who could deliver a course that would integrate smoothly into our curriculum. I contacted a consortium member university to explore the possibility of collaborating on this project with our university. As luck would have it, the very first institution I contacted had the faculty, equipment, facilities, and willingness to collaborate with our institution, me, and our technical staff. The administrators of each university worked out the contract language. I put technical media staff at each institution in touch with each other and began working with the faculty member at the remote site on the curricular and course design.

Determining the Measures. I decided that immediate and ongoing evaluative data would be collected at each class session, to allow for rapid intervention (if needed) by third-party observers (program faculty other than me), particularly regarding students at high risk for course failure, and to enable faculty to be part of the process. Previous course grades of students at both sites and final grades after completion of the research course delivered via teleconferencing would be compared and this data analyzed. Attendance would be monitored and compared to attendance of the same course in previous years.

Faculty observers were also enlisted to evaluate the instructor at the remote site and student participation in the class on-site. Student satisfaction would be measured through informal feedback (focus groups) and class question-and-answer sessions at the completion of each class. A formal, required course evaluation would be completed by students at course completion (once each semester). A student self-evaluation would also be requested by the instructor at the remote site on a weekly basis. Success level was set at 100 percent of the students meeting basic competency requirements (based on a minimum score of 70 percent) at the end of each semester, with zero student attrition rate. Finally, ongoing cost-effectiveness would be evaluated with a comparative cost-benefit analysis between current and previous course delivery costs. It was imperative that each cost center be identified, in order to sort out costs in terms of course design, delivery, and support. In other words, we needed separate line items for our course costs, technical support services costs, and administrative costs.

To secure appropriate feedback from a colleague at the university, I located someone who had experience in educational technology who had just transferred out of the academic affairs office to the university educational telecommunications department. He became my link to the administration, telecommunications, and our university teaching and learning enhancement center, as well as my sounding board for everything from understanding the technology to how to get my idea through the various committee levels of the approval process. His help was crucial, because this preliminary phase had to be completed prior to course implementation.

Implementing an Action and Observing the Results. Once the necessary administrative approvals were secured, articulation agreements were in place with the remote site, and technical support was confirmed at a local elementary school (after I realized that our university would not have all the equipment purchased in time), I began to market the course and its delivery mode internally to students and faculty two months in advance. The program was then implemented. Once the course began, I conducted interviews on a weekly basis with technical staff at the elementary school, our students, and the instructor (via e-mail). I also kept field notes during, and anecdotal records after, each class, recording my observations, notable incidents, suggestions, and anecdotes. I kept in weekly contact with my supportive colleague.

Evaluating the Results and Reflecting on the Project. Students' reactions were generally negative to the teleconferencing concept during the first week of class. The instructor was expending a tremendous amount of energy to deliver a quality course in an unfamiliar medium, using a course curricular structure unique to him. By the second week, a growing sense of student and instructor frustration was evident. A group teleconference revealed that the students wanted to be more interactive and less complacent. The instructor agreed, and allowed the students to provide input into the course format without modifying essential content. The effectiveness of this immediate identification and resolution of problems resulted in a highly effective, yet less formally structured class. The students were happy with their ability to provide direction for the course and the instructor's comfort level and presentation of material improved markedly by week three. Because the students had to enlist self-directed and group interaction skills as well as learn how to use electronic mail to communicate with the instructor, the Internet for computer conferencing, and an independently paced, computer statistical program for data analysis, their self-confidence in independent learning activities also improved.

Student feedback reflected an increase not only in skills, knowledge, and positive attitude toward research (course content), but also in their comfort level and skills in multimedia use for course requirements. I also observed that the students' group skills and self-reliance were enhanced as the semester progressed. Since this is a new initiative and the second part of the course has not yet been offered, I can't yet compare learner outcomes to previous years of traditional instructional methods. If preliminary evidence is accurate, however, the second phase of this course should prove cost-effective, provide secondary gains (student comfort with technology), and prompt our university to secure its own technical equipment sooner.

Action Research and Infection Control in a Hospital

Linda Ritchey

I am an infection control practitioner in a community-based hospital. My job focuses on reducing the risks of infection to hospitalized patients. The infection rate in the intensive care unit is most often the highest of all nursing units. Intensive care patients are seriously ill, and many need respiratory ventilators, arterial and venous lines, and surgery. Most infections are spread when nurses fail to wash their hands. I used action research to improve compliance on handwashing in the intensive care unit.

Understanding the Problem. Almost 150 years ago, in 1847, Ignac F. Semmelweis, then a young assistant to the professor of obstetrics at the University of Vienna, identified medical practices within hospitals as a major source and mode of the spread of infection. These infections, considered nosocomial (hospital-acquired), are developed within a hospital or are produced by microorganisms acquired during hospitalizations.

Nosocomial infections remain a significant problem for the health care system in the United States. At least 5 percent of patients will acquire an infection during their hospital stay, extending hospitalization by four days per infection, directly accounting for an estimated 60,000 deaths per year and an additional $10 billion spent on health care (Pillet, Herwald, and Massanari, 1992). Studies have demonstrated that pathogenic bacteria can be recovered from the hands of health care workers and transmitted to patients. Many experts have shown that hand carriage of organisms and subsequent contact may be the most important mechanism of nosocomial infection transmission in the intensive care unit (Maki, 1989).

Handwashing is the single most important procedure in the prevention of nosocomial infections, yet remains the most violated of all infection control procedures. Although intensive care units (ICUs) contain only 5 percent of hospital beds and care for less than 10 percent of hospitalized patients, infections acquired in these units account for more than 20 percent of nosocomial infections (Doebbeling, Stanley, and Sheetz, 1992).

Defining the Project. I used action research in my hospital with the intent of applying the findings to improve practices. Action research provides a means of testing new insights as they appear and observing systematically how each of these new insights affects and improves our practice. Nosocomial infections occur most frequently in the intensive care unit. Proper handwashing is recognized as the most important single procedure in the prevention of cross-infection in hospitals. Are health care workers washing their hands after each patient contact? Is lack of handwashing causing nosocomial infections in the intensive care unit? I decided that an observation of handwashing was needed to determine if handwashing practices were being followed in the intensive care unit at my hospital.

The handwashing issue seemed to lend itself to study and improvement through the action research cycle. I received permission to complete the study from hospital administration. I shared my plan for the study with the head nurse of the intensive care unit.

Determining the Measures. To measure the success of handwashing in the intensive care unit, I needed a definition of proper handwashing. I defined it as the washing of hands between patient contacts, using soap and water for a 10-second wash. The researcher made between 30 and 50 observations of handwashing practices at various times from 9:00 A.M. to 4:00 P.M. The dates of observation would include weekdays and weekends. The three items to be measured would be whether handwashing was done, length of handwashing procedure, and whether soap was used.

Implementing an Action and Observing the Results. Implementation, the observation of handwashing, was fairly simple to do. As an infection control practitioner, I frequently review charts and observe patients in the intensive care unit. For four days, I sat at the nurses station in ICU, in a location where I could observe the handwashing practices of the nurses. I varied the time of day and scattered the days to avoid nursing staff's awareness. Anonymity of the nursing staff was maintained as I made my observations.

Evaluating the Results and Reflecting on the Project. In reviewing the data collected on the 56 total observations, the following results were noted:

Handwashing done between patient contacts: 41 observations, 73 percent of total
Length of handwashing procedure: range 4–12 seconds, average 7 seconds
Soap used during handwashing: 50 observations, 89 percent of total.

I felt this study was valid in its findings. The results were shared with the head nurse of ICU as well as the physician chair of the hospital's infection control committee. Together we concluded that the results of these observations showed a need for improvement. The health care workers were negligent in not washing their hands between each patient contact, the length of the handwashing procedure was too short, and soap was not always used during handwashing.

The problem is that health care workers in the ICU are not washing their hands properly as noted by the observational study. During the second cycle of the action research process, I used the intervention of an educational program. I provided the program to all the ICU nurses. Within this program I reviewed the correct way to perform handwashing and offered the results of the first cycle of action research, which revealed the deficiencies discovered through the observational study.

A repeat observational study was completed one month following the educational program. The measures of the first observational study were repeated to allow a comparison between the first study and the second study. An ICU nurse was trained to complete the observational study because the ICU nurses would be suspicious of my presence in ICU a second time. The ICU nurse observer collected data on four different days and varied the observation time, completing 50 observations. In reviewing the data collected on the second study, the following results were noted:

Handwashing done between patient contacts: 46 observations, 92 percent of total
Length of handwashing procedure: range 6–15 seconds, average 9 seconds
Soap used during handwashing: 46 observations, 92 percent of total.

The outcome of the second study showed significant improvement, with a measurable difference from the first study. This use of defined measures provides generalizability; the study can be repeated. Education on proper handwashing was effective in improving handwashing practices.

Conclusion

Gary W. Kuhne

The six cases presented in this chapter present a strong argument for the usefulness of action research for adult educators. Although the six cases represent quite different practice contexts and issues, they demonstrate the problem-posing and problem-solving value of action research, as well as the usefulness of repeated cycles of research. As we saw in such varied settings as a museum, a church, a correctional facility, a homeless shelter, a university, and a hospital, the practical skills derived from the action research approach show great promise for resolving many of the issues faced by adult educators in practice. Whether you are a teacher, program designer, administrator, counselor, or volunteer, you can make use of this empowering approach to research. We hope you will be challenged by the cases presented and try action research the next time you try to address a practice problem or issue in your institution.

References

Doebbeling, B. N., Stanley, B. I., and Sheetz C. T. "Comparative Efficance of Alternative Handwashing Agents in Reducing Nosocomial Infections in Intensive Care Units." *New England Journal of Medicine,* 1992, *327,* 88–93.

Knowles, M. *The Modern Practice of Adult Education.* (2nd ed.) New York: Cambridge Books, 1980.

Maki, D. G. "The Use of Antiseptics for Handwashing by Medical Personnel." *Journal of Chemotherapy,* Apr. 1989, pp. 3–11.

McTaggart, R. "Principles for Participatory Action Research." *Adult Education Quarterly,* 1991, *41* (3), 168–187.

Pillet, D., Herwald, L., and Massanari, R. M. *The Intensive Care Unit.* New York: Little, Brown, 1992.

GARY W. KUHNE *is assistant professor of adult education at Pennsylvania State University and an evaluator/trainer in the Pennsylvania Action Research Network.*

DRUCIE WEIRAUCH *is on faculty in the Department of Professional Studies in Education, Indiana University of Pennsylvania, and is a trainer in the Pennsylvania Action Research Network.*

DAVID J. FETTERMAN *is associate pastor and minister of Christian education, First United Methodist Church, Murrysville, Pennsylvania, and a trainer in the Pennsylvania Action Research Network.*

RAIANA M. MEARNS *works in literacy education in Gettysburg, Pennsylvania, and is a former assistant administrator with the Pennsylvania Action Research Network.*

KATHY KALINOSKY *is an employment development administrator with Catholic Social Services in Wilkes-Barre, Pennsylvania, and a trainer in the Pennsylvania Action Research Network.*

KATHLEEN A. CEGLES *is assistant professor of physical therapy in the College of Sciences, Engineering, and Health at Gannon University in Erie, Pennsylvania.*

LINDA RITCHEY *is an infection control practitioner in a community-based hospital in Pennsylvania and a trainer in the Pennsylvania Action Research Network.*

*This chapter and the next form a dialogue intended to encourage
discussion in the field. Here, John Peters provides his comments on
action research and discusses the previous chapters of this sourcebook.*

Reflections on Action Research

John M. Peters

Many years ago, in a conversation with Myles Horton, founder of the Highlander Folk School in Tennessee, I asked what, for Myles, counted as learning
and what he considered to be the proper role of an adult educator. Myles
insisted that learning from one's own experience was the only way to learn,
and that the role of adult educator is to help people learn to learn from their
own experience, in the interest of changing society. Myles was never one to discuss "methods" or to claim one of his own. However, I had not yet let go of the
reins as a teacher, so I felt compelled to ask Myles, "What is 'wrong' with lecturing?" and other dumb questions. He replied, "Nothing. Lecturing is a great
way for the lecturer to learn."

The lecturer is the real learner in a classroom setting. Similarly, the
researcher is the one most likely to learn from a study of other people's activities. However, in both cases, the avowed intent of the lecturer and the
researcher is to help other people learn what the teacher knows or the
researcher discovers. Both are in the business of transmitting knowledge, disseminating results, and so forth.

If the researcher stands to gain more from a study of other peoples' lives
than the people whose lives are studied, how much might the *people* learn if
they were also the researchers? Moreover, how much more might they learn if
the focus of their inquiry was on their own lived experiences? They would be
learning from their experiences, through reflective inquiry. However, research
is usually thought to be the exclusive domain of "researchers"—distant, smart,
erudite, perhaps university-based people who have the power to name what is
to be known and how to know it. How, then, could ordinary mortals pretend
to act as researchers? Surely this is a job best left to experts.

This sourcebook presents a way of thinking about inquiry that blurs any
distinctions that might be made, in conventional terms, between the

researcher-expert and the people whose experiences are the subject of inquiry. In action research, while the researcher may be perceived as an outsider by a group of people conventionally known as "subjects," he or she is likely to be one of them. Or the group itself may be the researchers. The very name of this multimodal form of inquiry, *action research,* suggests that it is not stagnant, dull, removed, supportive of the status quo, or sterilized, free from the life of the moment and alien to those who live it. It is active, changing, engaging, alive. But it is not without its detractors, mainly those employed by research institutions. Meanwhile, even the most ardent advocates of action research continue to sort out issues that surround its uses in practical settings—issues related to purpose, power and control, ideology, roles, the nature of participation, and so forth.

The editors of this sourcebook, in the first two chapters, have addressed several such issues, and have thus provided a useful framework for further discussion of the nature and purposes of action research. The case descriptions in Chapter Three, authored by action researchers, provide a ground on which to stand as the discussion takes place. My job at this point is to reflect on what has been said and described thus far and to join the authors in further discussion of action research.

Naming Action Research

There is not just one way to do action research. There is not a single purpose shared by all action researchers. It is not research as usual. Best described, action research is a way in which people learn from their own and other peoples' experiences, by employing any number and variety of modes of systematic inquiry. More broadly still, action research represents a way of thinking about what knowledge is, whose it is, and how knowledge is created.

The editors of this sourcebook have called action research a mode of problem solving. That is what most writers on the subject say. Not many also say that action research can start from a point of just plain curiousness or interest, but why not? We adult educators like to say that we help people solve their problems. We intervene. And action research for the editors is an intervention. They say that people can use action research to learn to solve their problems. I agree, but would like to add that action research can be pursued in search of interesting new ways of learning and thus personal and professional development, and to contribute to theory that can be of general use to others, in addition to fixing what is broken.

Action research can also be used to create problems on purpose. This can be good or bad, depending on the motive of the researchers and the nature of their organization or community. Folks who want to change their organization's culture can study ways of doing so, and by way of action research set out to change that culture. But, this might not go down well with the status-quo politics. We can pick fights this way. We can get fired, or simply ostracized. Or jailed. Can action research be so rough? Was research ever meant to be so down and dirty? Talk about problems! Those who do participatory action research usually thrive on this kind of action.

The editors suggest that participatory action research is a species of action research. They also draw a line in this sourcebook, and choose not to step over it into the rough-and-tumble territory of participatory action research. They seem to prefer working in the domain of action research that is relatively safe, where the focus is on improving one's own practice, under one's own control of the situation. All this suggests a need to examine what is really intended by the editors and case writers in this book. Let's take a look at some possibilities.

Outcomes, Intended or Not

The shortest route to understanding what a researcher believes about research is to identify his or her intentions. What do they expect to accomplish, in terms of the outcomes of their research? There are several broad possibilities in the area of action research. Some outcomes have already been suggested by the editors in Chapter One. Others have been identified by authors of other books on action research. For me, they cluster in six categories.

First of all, nearly everyone says that action research is intended to improve one's practice, or way of doing work. Second, and relatedly, the practitioner should expect to improve his or her understanding of the practice. Third, as Kemmis and McTaggart (1988) point out, the outcomes should include an improvement in "the rationality and justice of (the practitioner's) own social or educational practices" (p. 5). Fourth, the outcome can be further theory development, including both "practical theory" and "formal theory." Fifth, the outcome might be further personal and professional development for the researcher. Sixth, the intended outcome might be a change in the system that forms the context for an action research project, or changes in related systems—a community, an organization, their cultures.

The editors draw their line between numbers five and six outcomes. They see number six as an outcome of participatory action research, to which they ascribe a special status. A privileged status, I think, judging from their description. This judgment comes from their argument that an adult educator might wish to engage in other forms of action research before stepping up to doing participatory action research. Surely the experience would do anyone some good, but I want to argue that an educator either does or does not have the political and philosophical attitude necessary to engage in action research for the principal purpose of changing society—to help people with little or no power to empower themselves. This is not some developmental stage one later achieves, just by doing some safer forms of action research first. The editors seem to believe that this form of action research is a different game from the others, and they're probably right. But to set it so far apart from what we otherwise feel comfortable with as educators is to fail to support those who genuinely pursue social change through education. And this can contribute to the ideological divide that the editors pointed out in Chapter One; I doubt that this was their intent.

Regarding those other five outcomes, it is easy enough to locate the cases in Chapter Three and the example in Chapter Two next to the first outcome on the above list—improvement in one's own practice. They also relate to the second outcome of better understanding one's practice. There is some evidence in the cases that the rationality and justice of practice were improved, or sought after, by some of the action researchers in Chapter Three. But, missing from all were outcomes having to do with personal and professional development or with theory development. I don't doubt that the researchers experienced some degree of personal and professional development, but I would have enjoyed knowing more about those experiences.

How might the action researcher seek to improve himself or herself in the process of doing action research? Much can be learned by engaging in this form of inquiry. Research skills can be developed. One's own assumptions about learning, about education, about people and organizations, and so forth can be accessed, examined, and perhaps changed. However, for this outcome to be realized, the action researcher needs to adopt a particularly self-reflective stance in his or her role as researcher. In essence, the researcher is a focus of the research, as is the process employed by the researcher. The editors correctly point out that action research is distinctive in terms of the researcher being a part of the study and not some distant, separate being "objectively" observing others in some cold, detached manner. However, they don't say much more about this very important aspect of action research, especially about what researchers can learn about themselves and the influence their own knowledge, intentions, and values have on the knowledge, intentions, and values of other participants in their study, and vice versa. The cases in Chapter Three display this oversight, as nearly all of them describe how a researcher or groups of researchers study their practice and its effect on other folks, but not how the other folks influence the researcher. I will say more about that later in this chapter, but first I need to say something about the nature of participation, collaboration, and involvement of others in their research.

Participation, Collaboration, and Involvement

Participation is a major theme in discussions about action research, as is involvement. And collaboration. However, these terms mean different things to different users. For example, McTaggart (1991) argues that participation does not mean the same thing as involvement. Drawing on a standard English dictionary definition, he defined *involve* as "to 'entangle . . . implicate . . . include'" and *participate* as "to 'share, take part'" (from Sykes, 1976, p. 804). McTaggart says that "authentic participation in research means sharing in the way research is conceptualized, practiced, and brought to bear on the life-world. It means ownership—a responsible agency in the production of knowledge and the improvement of practice. Mere involvement implies none of this and creates the risk of coop-tion and exploitation of people in the realization of the plans of others" (p. 171).

I agree with McTaggart's distinction. The two options implicate very different modes of inquiry. Throughout this sourcebook, *involvement* is the term most frequently used, or at least intended. For example, in Chapter Two, in Quigley's research with his own graduate class, involvement was what Quigley had in mind. He checked his plan with the students, told them what his intention was, and sought feedback from the students. He involved them. He was in control of the class. He made the principal decisions and checked them out with students. This was his plan, not theirs. No problem here, for Quigley said he wanted to involve his students in his plan. Had he said that his was some sort of participatory action research, his own actions might have been drastically changed. The decisions would have been the group's decisions, not his alone. The nature of the problem as Quigley named it might have been much different if the students had participated in posing it. The students and the professor would have jointly designed and conducted the study and interpreted the results. Participation, as McTaggart defines it, and as popular educators define it, would have changed the structure and intent of this teacher-directed and teacher-controlled piece of action research. But this was not Quigley's intent.

I believe that what some of us call participation is really involvement. We don't give up much control, although we say that the people affected by our research participate in doing the research. More often than not, "participants" provide a sounding board or are advisers, or simply go-alongs, politely cooperating with action researchers who are just one philosophical inch away from contradicting their own espoused beliefs about people participating in research that affects their lives.

A similar criticism can be leveled at the use of the term *collaboration*. The meaning of this term also varies greatly among its users. Yet the literature on action research lately is filled with the term, resulting in such labels as "collaborative action research," "collaborative inquiry," and "collaborative learning" (Brooks and Watkins, 1994; Oja and Smulyan, 1989). But what most writers call collaboration is in my judgement closer to cooperation. Collaboration, for me, means people laboring together with the intent of creating something. People engaged in collaborative learning are laboring together to produce knowledge (Peters and Armstrong, in press). They construct knowledge. This can benefit individual collaborators, the group, or both. On the other hand, *cooperative learning* (a very popular term these days, especially in the K–12 education world), does not mean the same thing as *collaborative learning* (Bruffee, 1993; Cranton, 1996). Cooperation means people working together to help each other out. Individual learning is the focus. There is not necessarily intent to construct new meaning together on the part of cooperating members of a group. Usually, in cooperative education, the teacher sets the agenda, tells the students what they are to learn, and the students work with one another in various ways to get the learning accomplished (Bosworth and Hamilton, 1994). There is a parallel distinction in terms of how collaborative action research is done. Most cases of so-called collaborative action research that I have read are actually cases of cooperation among people whose lives are being studied. So it is in the cases cited in this book, although, to be fair, I note that the authors do not make firm claims that they are doing collaborative work.

Collaborative research is to cooperative research as participation is to involvement in research. Each side of the ratio demands different things of the researcher, and the outcomes are usually different. It is time we action researchers reflect on what we mean by our use of these terms, and try to harmonize our espoused theory with our theory in practice.

Planning and Going with the Flow

The editors propose a four-step approach to action research: planning, acting, observing, and reflecting. These steps, similar to those proposed by Kemmis and McTaggart (1984) and still earlier by Lewin (1948), are intended to be helpful to readers interested in how to do action research. These steps are broken down into even more specific directions, which the editors provide in their action research planner (see the Appendix to Chapter Two). The model involved can be a useful guide for first-time researchers and a good reminder to experienced researchers. However, the model should be just that—a guide. To follow a step-by-step, recipe-like procedure is to miss the point of action research. The point has to do with the fluid, construct-as-you-go process involved.

The editors point out, correctly, that action research should proceed in an iterative manner, thereby agreeing with many other writers on the topic (Oja and Smulyan, 1989). Most say that the process, whether stepwise or not, should be repeated in cycles, such that action leads to reflection, which leads to further, more informed action, which leads to more reflection, and so forth. This cycle of action-reflection-action is basic to most models of action research that I have examined. The fluid, ever-changing, and unpredictable nature of the actions involved is basic to most accounts of what happens in action research projects. The actions change, and one reason that they change is that the action researcher makes changes in his or her practice on the basis of reflective thinking about results obtained from earlier actions. Predicting results from an action-reflection-action cycle is especially problematic if other participants are truly part of the research. When people research collaboratively, they co-construct their reality. And reality shifts.

Kuhne and Quigley's description of the action research planner contains highly-detailed guides for manipulating all foreseeable contingencies of an action research project. Detailed questions are posed for decision making at every step of the way. However, there are some very curious uses of language in the questions. Even though Quigley and Kuhne seem to favor authentic involvement, if not participation, on the part of people whose lives are being studied, Kuhne's questions suggest a researcher-controlled approach. Consider these questions, for example: In the planning phase, "How can you intervene with a new strategy or approach to see if it would make a difference? What can you do differently? How will you do it? Can you conduct this project in a way that allows you to manage and observe the activities? How will you manage the effects that will result?" In the action phase, "Are you staying true to the initial plan? Are you collecting the data the way you said you would?" In the reflection phase, "How could you repeat this intervention (or have it repeated) to develop more validity?"

Chapter Two describes Quigley's own action research project as follows: " [Quigley] did decide to try the mini-lecture. He decided to tell the class about the change and get their input as to which teaching method they liked best after a two-month trial period." Finally, in describing some methodologies that an action researcher might employ, Chapter Two says this about interviews: "Interviews conducted by you or perhaps by another person—*which often improves objectivity*— can be invaluable" (my emphasis). In describing possible design options, Chapter Two suggests the possibility of control groups being used in "inductive experimentation" as an action research option. For example, if given a chance to do so, what would happen if a "control group" of adult participants posed the research problem differently from the problem as the researcher saw it?

So, what do all the above samples of language, taken from the description of the editors' action research model say to the reader? To me, they say that the editors' stepwise action research model is essentially a positivist approach to inquiry. I don't think this is what the editors intended to convey, however. What's more, using Quigley's selection of Habermas's work as a frame for understanding action research (see Chapter One), the editors' externally controlled planning model clearly falls in the philosopher's "technical" category, not the "practical" category, as the editors claim it does. In their description of the model, there is a "truth" to be pursued, an "actual" problem involved, and there is a cause-effect relationship between the researcher's intervention and the expected measurable results. This is a classic problem-solving model that guides the adult educator along an instrumentalist approach to intervening in others peoples' lives—with their permission, of course.

Six Cases, Plus One

Chapter Three contains six cases of action research, which are useful in illustrating the editors' ideas about action research. An additional case is cited in Chapter Two. I analyzed the cases with the aim of identifying themes that would further my own understanding of action research and eliciting the editors' reactions to the same. Five themes surfaced from the analysis: adherence to the editors' model of action research, the relationship of the researcher to the focus of the inquiry, the incidence of reflective thinking, evidence of follow-up or cycles of inquiry, and the nature of involvement or participation in the cases.

The case descriptions were organized according to the four-part model suggested by Quigley and Kuhne: planning, acting, observing, and reflecting. All descriptions fit neatly into these four categories of research activity. However, what is not clear is whether the researchers actually followed the four-step process as they planned and conducted their research project, in the order of the steps proposed by the editors. Knowing whether or not the process actually occurred in a stepwise fashion would be helpful to readers interested in using this guide in their own research.

It is clear that all of the steps are included to a greater or lesser degree in most action research projects, although interpretations of the steps may vary among users. For example, observing may take many forms and implicate different ways the observer might position himself or herself with respect to other participants in the research. It is also unlikely that action research projects can actually be conducted in the tight linear order of steps suggested by the model (the editors do say that the steps are not necessarily done in the order presented in Figure 2.1). I invite the editors' comments on this observation.

On the second theme, the relationship of the researcher to the focus of inquiry, two different forms of relationship stood out for me. One involved the researcher inquiring into his or her own immediate practice, and the other involved the researcher inquiring into more broadly organizational concerns. The cases that reflect the first form are Quigley's project, the museum project, the corrections project, and the homeless shelter project. The religious education project, the higher education project, and the hospital education project illustrate the second form.

The difference between these two forms mainly concerns how close the researcher is to the researched. In the first form, the problem is of direct concern to the researcher, and his or her own efforts are addressed by the research. For example, the literacy teacher in the homeless shelter faced a problem of low attendance in her own classes. Quigley needed to make adjustments in his own teaching technique. On the other hand, the projects in the second form involved the practitioners in doing something that would more nearly benefit the organizations in which they were employed or organizations that somehow were connected to them. For example, the hospital education case involved a problem of disease control that was of concern to the hospital in which the researcher worked. While the researcher/infection control practitioner had responsibility for training nurses in the practice of proper sanitation procedures, her own direct practical concern was not with disease control per se, as much as nurse training. It was through nurse training that the incidence of handwashing was changed and the hospital benefited.

I would enjoy a discussion of the differences, if any, that such forms of researcher relationships might have on the way the researcher approaches inquiry. To suggest one possibility, the difference might affect the willingness of the researcher to reflect on how his or her own assumptions enter into the inquiry. If the focus of inquiry is of direct concern to the researcher—for example, his or her own classroom behavior—the researcher might be more apt to be self-critical in reflecting on research results compared to situations in which the researcher is instrumental in helping the organization change. Do the editors perhaps have opinions on this?

The concern with researcher assumptions relates to the next theme, the incidence of reflective thinking in each project. Although all projects included a reflection step, some researchers were more reflective than others. What is of greater concern to me, however, is not what happened at the end of each project (the reflection stage, according to the model), but what happened during the project, and how critical the researchers were of themselves. The focus of reflective thinking for all of the researchers was on the method and results, especially the latter. This is little different from what any researcher might do. However, in action research, the researcher is acknowledged to be a vital part of the phenomena studied. Thus, the researcher should be as much a focus of reflection as the method and results.

An illustration of the importance of critical self-reflection in the research process can be found in the museum education case. The program specialist clearly believed that the proper mode of adult education is one that is learner-centered and experience-based, whereas the instructors with whom she worked were, in her judgment, overly subject-centered and fond of lecturing. While the researcher's assumptions about proper adult teaching methods are widely shared by other adult educators, they were obviously not as strongly held by the instructors whose behavior the researcher sought to change. Such a difference in assumptions easily factors into the dynamics of the researcher-subject relationship, and ought to be a part of what is to be understood by both researcher and participants. In the museum case, the research problem was defined in terms of the researcher's assumptions about how adults learn best. (Note that the instructors were not directly involved in posing this problem.) My concern is not with the particular assumptions held by this researcher, but with the need for any researcher to examine his or her assumptions about any aspect of his or her research. A critical examination of one's assumptions could result in a different definition of the research problem, selection of method, or interpretation of findings. All the cases in Chapter Three lacked this feature of the action research process.

The fourth theme involves one of the basic assumptions of the editors' model of action research, the provision for cycles of inquiry. Only two of the case descriptions included more than one cycle of inquiry (the homeless shelter case and Allan's case). The circumstances of each of the other cases could have prevented additional research cycles from being carried out, but there were missed opportunities nevertheless. Although the relationship is not a perfect one, the more cycles that are involved, the more learning opportunities are made available to researchers and participants alike. The iterative nature of action research as defined by the editors suggests a constructive process of knowledge production, and the potential of the process is limited only by the willingness of the researchers and others involved to construct new understandings from their experience.

The fifth and last theme relates to the extent of involvement or participation of other people in the researcher's project. The difference between participation and involvement has been discussed in this chapter, and in terms of that difference, it seemed safe to conclude that all the cases in this book involved other people, but the other people were not participants in the research process. In all cases, researchers consulted with other people, including those whose actions were studied, but in no case did the others participate fully in the definition of the research problem and the selection of methodologies. There was evidence of something more closely akin to participation at the reflection stage of each case, when results were discussed with people who were affected by the research. However, as pointed out at the beginning of this chapter, the editors and the case researchers did not set out to do participatory action research, and the examples of their work reflect this intent. It is not possible to know from these examples what would have been different about the projects if researchers had brought others into the problem-posing stage before they designed and implemented their research projects.

Conclusion

I have attempted to respond to the editors' ideas about action research and to the cases that illustrate the use of their action research model. Their ideas, model, and cases certainly provide a great deal of useful material for novice and experienced action researchers to consider in the context of their own practices. What I have said in response reflects my own beliefs and experiences, and I am naturally open to criticism from others, including the editors. I expect to learn even more from this exercise when I read the editors' views of my views.

References

Bosworth, K., and Hamilton, S. J. (eds.). *Collaborative Learning: Underlying Processes and Effective Techniques*. New Directions for Teaching and Learning, no. 59. San Francisco: Jossey-Bass, 1994.

Brooks, A., and Watkins, K. E. (eds.) *The Emerging Power of Action Inquiry Technologies*. New Directions for Adult and Continuing Education, no. 63. San Francisco: Jossey-Bass, 1994.

Bruffee, K. *Collaborative Learning: Higher Education, Interdependence, and the Authority of Knowledge*. Baltimore: Johns Hopkins University Press, 1993.

Cranton, P. "Types of Group Learning." In S. Imel (ed.), *Learning in Groups: Exploring Fundamental Principles, New Uses, and Emerging Opportunities*. New Directions for Adult and Continuing Education, no. 71. San Francisco: Jossey-Bass, 1996.

Kemmis, S., and McTaggart, R. (eds.). *The Action Research Planner*. Geelong, Australia: Deakin University Press, 1984.

Kemmis, S., and McTaggart, R. (eds.). *The Action Research Planner*. (2nd ed.) Geelong, Australia: Deakin University Press, 1988.

Lewin, K. *Resolving Social Conflicts*. New York: HarperCollins, 1948.

McTaggart, R. "Principles for Participatory Action Research." *Adult Education Quarterly*, 1991, *41* (3), 168–187.

Oja, S., and Smulyan, L. *Collaborative Action Research: A Developmental Approach*. London: Falmer Press, 1989.

Peters, J., and Armstrong, J. *Facilitating Collaborative Learning*. San Francisco: Jossey-Bass, in press.

Sykes, J. (ed.). *The Concise Oxford Dictionary of Current English*. Oxford, England: Oxford University Press, 1976.

JOHN M. PETERS *is professor of adult education at the University of Tennessee, Knoxville.*

The editors respond to the questions and concerns raised by John Peters in Chapter Four, then provide a conclusion.

"A Condition That Is Not Yet": Reactions, Reflections, and Closing Comments

B. Allan Quigley, Gary W. Kuhne

Perhaps the only thing more interesting than research itself is the controversy that research can create. Our hope for this sourcebook is that it will foster discussion among university researchers, practitioners, and learners. In fostering this hoped-for discussion, we believe that John Peters has touched on some extremely important points in his chapter—some which we agree with, some which we do not agree with—as would be expected.

Bourdieu once observed, "Reality is not an absolute . . . it differs with the group to which one belongs" (1971, p. 195). It will be seen that reality differs to varying degrees between Peters and us, but in ways that we believe have helped crystallize many of the key questions that arise from this sourcebook. We have tried to highlight and discuss these questions and are indebted to Peters for his valuable contributions to this text.

Following are a number of the implications that arise from our dialogue here. There are surely more, but perhaps these can provide a starting place for the discussion we hope will follow.

What Is Intended?

We can begin with some questions: Can researchers really know what they intend? On what basis can researchers both accept and learn from the research intentions of others? With reference to the intentionality framework in Chapter One (Table 1.2), had the Peters critique in the last chapter been written by someone who works mainly with positivist empiricism, we would speculate that the earlier chapters and action research would have been criticized for lack of scientific rigor. Perhaps it is good that it did not. As discussed in Chapter One, it was the "lack of scientific rigor" criticism that discredited and killed interest in action research for several decades in the public school system. In other words, if the commentary had come from the empiricist "technical" category, the first concern regarding rigor would probably have been the lack of "necessary" distance between the expert researcher and the subjects being researched. Since the constant concern is with control in the positivist paradigm, further questions would surely have been raised regarding the control of variables in action research—or the lack of control, more exactly. In fact, Merriam and Simpson (1984) observed that action research has limitations "because it lacks external and internal controls" (p. 108) and therefore "has little generalizability" (p. 108). It would be in this tradition that, as Peters facetiously put it, one might hear the comment, "How, then, could ordinary mortals pretend to act as researchers? Surely, this is a job best left to experts."

Those in the tradition of positivist research often see their own research intents alone as appropriate and would probably reject entirely the two other categories described in our framework in Table 1.2. We saw Blunt (1994) in Chapter One, for instance, arguing for a "hard" and "soft" categorization of research. However, it is this empiricist group of researchers in the historic professionalization tradition that has had to gradually come to accept forms of qualitative research. We hope that forms of qualitative collaborative research such as action research, with "practitioners-as-mere-mortals" involved, will come to be more fully accepted in the production and ownership of knowledge as well.

By contrast, for those who work primarily in the "emancipatory" category of the intentionality framework (such as John Peters, who informs his discussion in Chapter Four with reference to Myles Horton of Highlander Research and Education Center) the concern would be the exact opposite. The issue in the emancipatory category is not empirical objectivity or loss of control; the issue here is degrees of emancipation or concern that the researcher retains *too much* control. Emancipatory research, as discussed in Chapter One, seeks to empower the learners first and to do so from the very outset, with full group involvement at every step. This assumption behind most of the emancipatory tradition was indicated in the intentionality framework (Table 1.2). The researcher in the emancipatory category should, of course, improve his or her practice, but the improvement should mainly come in the context of practitioner empowerment, in the sense that "the rationality and justice of [the practitioner's] own social or educational practices" should improve—Peters' third principle (p. 131).

To further make the point of how both of these categories of research have their own sets of imperatives, one can substitute a few words into Merriam and Simpson's (1984) earlier positivist criticism of action research and see the emancipatory argument at work: "Action research has limitations because it does not 'relinquish' external and internal controls." Most of the methodologies outside of the emancipatory stream are limited not because they have "insufficient generalizability" but because they have "insufficient 'empowerability.'"

However, if the response in Chapter Four were from someone working in the "practical" category of Table 1.2—where we believe action research and the majority of interpretivist methods (Merriam, 1991) can be found—the first concern would probably have been the extent of professional knowledge gain and personal growth of the practitioner (Schön, 1983). Those working in the practical category typically seek to create long-term benefits for all concerned—including the employing institution—by focusing first on the practitioner. In this process, action research and many of the methods in the practical category are not intended to seek generalized "truths," nor are they typically intended to seek deep structural or political change. Those working in the practical category seek to clarify and inform the researcher or practitioner-researcher for the benefit of his or her practice and to stimulate and advise other practitioners and researchers in order that knowledge from their studies may be shared. In this process, most practitioner-researchers hope other practitioners will try what they found for the good of the learners and the good of the field.

Looking at the wider ramifications of this attention to practitioners and their practice over either generalizability or social change, the distinctions between the technical, practical, and emancipatory categories, as Habermas allows, are not merely mechanical. They are founded on ideological difference. While the distinctions among these three were shown to be poorly understood in the K–12 literature because theirs is largely an institutional history, the history of adult education made it very clear that our differing research approaches have different purposes and different foci. These arise from a long history of varying purposes and ideological division in adult education dating at least to the two traditions of reform and professionalization discussed by Cotton in 1964.

Adult educators are no strangers to diversity of purpose and differences in approach. Courtney (1989) has observed that this field will never "speak with one voice" (p. 13). We hope that researchers in the three categories will be willing to both accept others' intentions and learn from each other across the lines of ideology. Learning from one another is what constitutes a healthy, robust profession (Cervero, 1988).

However, change comes incrementally to the basically conservative mainstream of this field, as mentioned in Chapter One. We hope that action research (a "safe" form of collaborative research, as Peters calls it) will become an even more acceptable means of knowledge production over time. As discussed earlier in this sourcebook, we also hope that it will be the next significant incremental step in the category of practical research (see Table 1.2).

Clarifying Intentions in Research

Turning to the more specific questions raised by Peters, an analysis of his language indicates that he too sometimes suggests what he actually intends while saying something else. Sometimes he sees the participatory action research that he is so invested in as distinctly different from action research; at other times he wants action research to be participatory research. His third and sixth categories of outcomes for action research, for example, seem like examples of wanting action research to be for participatory research purposes. The point made earlier in Chapter Three was that there are times when action research is not appropriate as a methodology and participatory research might be the better approach. Horton himself allowed that social change is not for everyone (Moyers, 1982); however, for Peters it seems that virtually every practitioner problem, if seen with sufficient depth of critical analysis, can lend itself to an increase in "the rationality and justice of (the practitioner's) own social or educational practices"—his third type of outcome. For him and many working in the emancipatory category, virtually every question inherently provides an exciting opportunity for "a change in the system that forms the context for an action research project, or changes in related systems"—his sixth type of outcome.

Like Freud, who advised that a cigar is "sometimes just a cigar," our view is that, for most of the practitioners we are thinking of, a technique for teaching, a strategy for tutoring, or a system for administering, may in fact be only the mundane practice problem that it seems, nothing more. Notwithstanding Peters' comment that "surely the experience would do anyone some good," like it or not, our experience tells us that some practitioners are unwilling or are incapable of "stepping up to" participatory research as John Peters advocates. Certainly the positivists in the technical category would feel just as strongly that the experience of "valid scientific research" would do anyone some good, too. This is a pure value judgment.

Our position is that what we do in action research varies with the problem, the practitioner, and the circumstance. It varies with what the practitioner is comfortable with. And frankly, we would fear that the universal experience Peters is advocating as doing "anyone some good" might actually do some practitioners and some programs some harm.

Peters says he would have preferred that we had not set the ideological paradigms of action research and participatory research "so far apart." However, as discussed in Chapter One, adult education's history shows us an ideological division that has existed for almost a century. Those "folks who want to change their organization's culture," as Peters refers to them, and those who claim they are willing to be "fired," "ostracized," or "jailed" in the process have a truly admirable ideology (although it often seems there is an unusually large group of tenured professor who advocate this from a safe "theoretical" distance). However, this admirable group is a long way from those researchers who spend their time worrying about chi-squares and advocate positivist goals. For our part, we are trying to build the centrist's position in the research framework with a "practical" category that we believe contains the majority of interpretivist research methods, borrows from both sides of the framework, and can lead outward to increased interest in emancipatory or positivist research. Coming from the professional paradigm, we hope to benefit practitioners first, since they sustain the field and are key to improving it. We include institutions where adult education practitioners work, whereas the emancipatory category typically does not, and we see learners, the field, and society as the beneficiaries of action research by practitioners.

We seek the middle ground, however structurally functional, naively humanist, or scientifically misguided this may seem to some on the other sides of the intentionality table. As for naïveté, we hope neither to widen nor close the century-old gap of ideology that has prevailed in adult education. Rather, we would suggest it naive to think that this small sourcebook would affect the long-standing history one way or another, as Peters cautions us in his chapter. In short, Peters champions oppressed learners, the empiricists champion science. We choose to champion those who do so much of the difficult, under-recognized day-to-day work of adult education—the practitioners.

Courtney observes that "adult education can play a central role in enfranchising all adults . . . so that everyone has a voice" (p. 13). We are trying to speak first to those adult educators who are the unromantic heroes of our field, to those who receive so little social or professional recognition and who enjoy virtually no practical assistance from academics. We believe in the practitioners—in their critical insights, their judgments, and their best decisions for improving this varied field of adult education. We also believe that collaboration through action research provides a humanistic, adult-helping-adult decision-making process with great accessibility to practitioners who wish to learn from practice and engage in knowledge production. As Horton put it, "you don't teach people things, since they're adults; you help them learn. And insofar as you learn how people learn, you can help" (Moyers, 1982, p. 250).

Exploring the differences of intent that arise from Peters' comments, we find it significant that Peters turns to Kemmis and McTaggart (1984) for the distinctions he makes between participation and involvement. Kemmis and McTaggart frequently advocate an intent different in quality, if not in kind, than ours. Several times in his chapter, Peters observes that what the eight researchers in this book did was possibly not what they intended. More precisely, he suggests that we often intended to create "participation," or mistakenly believed we actually experienced participation, but that we were often a bit naive in all this, since we frequently had the mere "involvement" of participants. We had participants' cooperation and consent, at most.

While it is true that all eight of us may be naive (arguably a helpful limitation if one is to aspire to publish in this field), it is not as clear as Peters suggests that we repeatedly failed to do what we intended—quite the contrary. Every case study shown earlier in this sourcebook makes the researcher's intent quite clear—namely, to conduct action research as defined, discussed, and described in the first three chapters. Our intent was not to conduct participatory research or participatory action research.

We do not insist that every action researcher should or can always have every participant in his or her study engaged in the analysis and definition of the problem from the very problem-posing outset. Such participation may be unfeasible or, in some circumstances, even inadvisable. It is a matter of the practitioner-researcher's judgment as to where to turn for the most meaningful input for his or her perceived problem in the problem-posing stage and, indeed, in every stage. Peters seems to assume that learners are a natural check on the practitioner-researcher. The types of settings we are thinking of and the purposes we have in mind would say this is not a universal truth. He seems to say we need to mistrust institutions and their representatives. We do not always agree.

Participant involvement can grow to higher and higher degrees of participation during a project, or the opposite. Much depends on the problem and the participants. We have suggested that knowledgeable, sympathetic colleagues typically are the best people to consult first in the problem-posing stage. In saying this, we realize that many practitioners, such as literacy tutors, work completely alone in remote areas with no colleagues close at hand. We realize that some institutional settings may allow for only periodic input from colleagues. It is for this reason that Table 1.2 says "individual or group basis" under the practical category, whereas it says only "group basis" under the emancipatory category. Therefore, action research may entail "mere" participant involvement in problem posing or any of the other steps, as Peters so correctly observes, but research in the emancipatory category needs all of the group participating all of the time. This is just not practical in many of the situations we are talking about.

Looking more closely at the case studies in Chapter Three, in David Fetterman's case in the church setting, his problem posing led to the creation of a task force chosen from the members of the congregation—full "participants"— to identify, analyze, and brainstorm possible interventions for the problem of low participation in the education program. His intent was to increase participation and build ownership of the problem. In the homeless shelter where Kathy Kalinosky worked, many potential participants were women who stayed in their rooms and, for understandable reasons, would not interact as a larger group. Like Fetterman, Kalinosky managed to convene a task force to initiate ideas for an intervention. She too sought problem ownership and she too succeeded in obtaining full participation of the task force members in both the problem-posing and the action phases. To try to engage many more of the participants early on would have been extremely difficult. The principle of "all the participants all the time" would have been so impractical that neither project would have gotten off the ground.

Different problems call for different strategies. As described in Chapter Two, Quigley's attempts to discuss the complaint of too much reading had led to the suggestion of cutting back on the readings—an intervention he had tried several times but one that had repeatedly failed to help either the instructor or the learners. In that case, learners in his introductory class understandably had trouble imagining alternatives when it was, after all, their first graduate class. This may be seen as similar to Kathleen Cegles' situation, where no one in her university was aware of or had experience with distance education. As it happened, Quigley got his suggestion for mini-lectures from a senior graduate student. Cegles got her ideas from her own experience in an adult education doctoral program. In Raiana Mearns' case with volunteers at the prison, her intent was to see if college students would be successful tutors. To brainstorm with either the inmates or the newly arrived volunteers in the problem-posing phase was not practical. Rather, Quigley, Cegles, and Mearns each sought involvement of the participants at the start of the implementation phase and hoped the action of the project and the reflective stage would help all to learn from what the action science people call "theory-in-use" (Argyris, 1982).

Cegles in the higher education setting, Weirauch in the museum setting, and to a lesser extent, Quigley in his classroom study, all intended to bring about change in the existing institutional culture. Despite Peters' observation about "safe" research, the first two took considerable risks in the context of their institution's culture and purposes. Faculty at Cegles' university might have asked if they were becoming redundant; Weirauch was attempting to effect change among some highly qualified scholars who were donating their time to the museum. Neither occupied particularly powerful positions, yet, even if it did not come out in the written case studies, they would each would attest that they took greater risks than their predecessors or colleagues. This willingness to take risks is surely to the credit of the practitioner-researchers, but we also believe there is something about the systematic process of problem posing in action research that enables and encourages researchers to take risks in their institutions when others may not.

Finally, Linda Ritchey's hospital case was an exception to even our loose guidelines, since the participants did not and could not know there was an experiment going on. She had the permission of the nursing supervisor but no involvement with the nurses in the intensive care unit. Despite what must seem like heresy to emancipatory researchers, satisfaction for those of us in the practical stream comes with knowing that the ICU infection levels decreased so dramatically through this study and the practitioner-researcher's later cycles of it—that Linda assuredly saved patients' lives. What works, works. And as Peters himself rightly observed, "there is not just one way to do action research."

"Depending on the *motive* of the researchers" (emphasis added), as Peters puts it, we see that there are indeed intentional differences in how researchers approach problems. We see different levels of participation and involvement at various stages of action research. And we see that there are some problems action researchers should not attempt, just as there are undoubtedly some that empirical and emancipatory researchers should avoid. Thus, two larger questions arise from this dialogue: Can researchers know what they intend? On what basis can they accept and learn from the research intentions of others?

Can We Know What We Intend?

We propose that researchers might benefit from answering the following questions in the problem-posing stage (a stage common to all research) before settling on a method of inquiry or beginning a project:

Who do you intend to be the first beneficiary of this research? The second? The third? Others? Who should be involved in this early stage of problem definition and brainstorming? How have you arrived at this set of answers? Are you convinced that your method is adequate to the problem posed?

What do you intend to be the first level of change? The second? The third? What are other levels or areas you intend to change now or in later cycles? How have you arrived at this set of answers? Are you convinced that your method is adequate to the problem posed?

Is there an ethical risk when action researchers impose their own "solutions" on participants? Those in the positivist stream will argue that researchers should never bring a preconceived solution to research or seek to impose one. By the technical category's definition, arriving at preconceived solutions would not be research. A researcher from this paradigm merely brings a hypothesis to test. Of course, many in the other research schools have argued that scientific neutrality is a myth (Guba and Lincoln, 1981). Humans are not neutral; they make choices. For many in the emancipatory stream, the empirical researchers are just allowing status-quo injustices to continue by claiming "neutrality." For emancipatory researchers, the "neutral positivist" researchers are just choosing to turn a blind eye in the name of science. The atomic bomb might be a case in point.

Both practical and emancipatory categories of researchers intend to intervene, as Peters says. Unlike the positivists, we do intend to bring about change, and we do intend to create improvement. Since so much of the dialogue between Peters and us revolves around intentions, it is worth reminding ourselves of the saying, "The road to hell is paved with good intentions." There are serious ethical considerations in research—action research and participatory research included.

However, it not always easy to see where Peters comes down on ethics in this brief exchange, since he says, "Folks who want to change their organization's culture can study ways of doing so, and by way of action research set out to change that culture." Yet in the case of the museum setting, one of at least three where the researcher set out to change a teaching culture, Peters is suddenly cautious. It is not challenge to the status quo, but who initiates it. A critical examination of one's assumptions could result in a different definition of the research problem, selection of method, or interpretation of findings, as Peters says. And he is quite correct here. Researchers must conduct a critical examination of their assumptions going into research. We hope that the questions presented earlier in the sourcebook will be of assistance to future action researchers. However, in the museum case and each of the others as well, each researcher *had* critically examined his or her assumptions about their research project—alone, with colleagues where possible, and with all of the participants when appropriate.

Peters raised concerns about the museum setting case study specifically. In that case, Drucie Weirauch, the researcher, had examined her assumptions about teaching; she had carefully analyzed the problem; she had reviewed the situation with colleagues and had decided that this was an area for practice improvement that might help the faculty, the students, and the institution. She examined the depth of the institutional and faculty critique she was comfortable with in the context of her professional responsibilities, and she came to the conclusion that interactive "andragogical" teaching might be more effective with adults than the lecturing method she had inherited. As Horton says in the opening of Peters' chapter, "Lecturing is a great way for the lecturer to learn."

The point Peters seems to suggest is that, by taking leadership, Weirauch may have been imposing a preconceived solution on the participants and was perhaps uncritically manipulating them toward acceptance of what she wanted them to do. Peters wonders if she should have engaged in more critical reflection and early problem posing with the faculty before launching into her project. Peters is quite right that imposition of solutions and biases is a distinct possibility in action research (and no less so in participatory research). However, Weirauch herself commented, "To help the instructors see the importance of learners' needs and experiences, it was important that I not hypocritically posture as the expert; the teachers must be involved in the process." Remembering that faculty considered themselves professionals in their subject areas and many had told her they wanted to be better teachers, Weirauch made it possible for them to discover a problem as seen by the learners in their lecture halls. The faculty could have opted out of her action research project at any time and had the opportunity to discuss the implications of her project in a formative way at any time.

Weirauch hoped to gain the involvement of an otherwise resistant teaching staff using a tactful, practical approach. "Approval was . . . obtained from all of the instructors. I sent them a letter describing the revised [evaluation] form *and its intended use* [emphasis added] for professional instructional development. I explained how it would give them better information about students' abilities in relation to the instructor's goals for the class and also provide individuals' expectations and goals. I also explained that by providing the methods, techniques, and materials for the form, they would be able to learn what is effective. *I invited the instructors to call me for clarification; several did*" (emphasis added). Weirauch depended on the teachers, the students, and a colleague observer to ensure that the project was a wide open process. She was very much engaged with all of these people throughout this project—particularly during the reflection stage, as Peters noted.

We see through this and all of the case studies that there are both functional and ethical issues in every action research project. Functionally, Weirauch felt she could only begin to change the teaching culture by tactfully trying to raise the critical consciousness of the faculty to the point where they could accept the possibility that there might be a problem. Ethically, she wanted to avoid hypocritical posturing, so she carefully set a process in motion that raised the critical awareness of all her participants with their full knowledge. She ensured access to further information from her, and every teacher had the opportunity to drop out. The fact that all were encouraged to have continual dialogue among themselves, with their students, and with Weirauch (for the first time) and all were volunteers in the project indicates that Weirauch was not imposing "solutions"; rather, she was using a consciousness-raising technique that Freire (1973) himself advocated.

All of Weirauch's risk taking may or may not have led to the andragogical outcome she personally wanted (and that Peters wanted, too). Her project might have failed, and she was prepared to accept that possibility. But many instructors chose to begin problem posing. Many took a different teaching tack. A dialogue on teaching had begun.

Some Ethical Questions

Following are the larger ethical questions that emerge from this discussion and that may help expand the first set given earlier:

Have all the research participants not only given their consent but been involved in the problem-posing process? If the answer is "not very much," you might ask how you have arrived at this particular course of action. Could this be a mistaken identification of the problem or intervention? Are colleagues' suggestions adequate in this case? Would the reflection stage benefit from more active participation, not simply involvement, early on?

Can every step be ethically justified? Have alternative interventions been discussed with participants, knowledgeable colleagues, and supervising management? Can every participant get further explanation about this project at any time? Not only that, but does every participant know that he or she can drop out at any point? Finally, are you convinced your method is adequate to the problem posed?

Can action researchers really engage in critical self-reflection? The model for action research presented in Chapter Two places problem posing at the beginning of each cycle. And we said that the purpose of action research is professional and, implicitly, personal growth. However, Peters has also observed that "missing from all [the cases] were outcomes having to do with personal and professional development or with theory development." He adds, "I don't doubt that the researchers experienced some degree of personal and professional development, but I would have enjoyed knowing more about those experiences." Here is a point that is not taken from a participatory research perspective; it is truly one of the important steps in action research itself. On the basis of our own professional development model, we would reply that, to the extent that Peters or any reader feels this area was not covered thoroughly enough, we have created a limitation in this text. Considerable professional and personal growth has taken place for us all, and this may not have been sufficiently discussed here. Professional and personal development are key elements of action research. We would do it differently now and include more on personal and professional growth; however, unlike the real world, there are rarely second and third cycles in the frozen-in-time world of publishing.

Suffice it to say that each of us as action researchers did experience both personal and professional growth as a result of our projects, and as a result of later cycles and later action research work, we have all continued to explore and learn more on our given issues and others, in the tradition of action research. Drucie Weirauch has since left the museum and, in addition to her many other professional activities, is now engaged in training and mentoring some twenty new action researchers in greater Pittsburgh as part of our statewide action research network in Pennsylvania, which is entering its third year of operation. David Fetterman is still at his church, which has increased attendance in religious education. He is continuing with further cycles of his project and is training and mentoring new action researchers with our project in northwestern Pennsylvania.

Kathy Kalinosky is no longer working with the homeless shelter; unfortunately, the homeless shelter where she worked was closed, as she mentioned in Chapter Three. Nevertheless, she has continued in literacy work and in helping adults find employment. Kathy is also training and mentoring new action researchers in our action research project in northeast Pennsylvania. Linda Ritchey is still working in the intensive care unit and has been working to make the results of her project known in the health field (a real opportunity for theory building). She, too, trains and mentors action researchers with our project in south central Pennsylvania. Raiana Mearns left the corrections area but not literacy education. She is a former administrator with our Pennsylvania Action Research Network and took part in a presentation with us at a state conference on adult education. In this presentation, we discussed what we have learned over the past two years of our statewide project. Meanwhile, Kathy Cegles has continued to develop the distance education teaching model at her university and has received positive evaluations from all involved.

As for us, the mini-lecture project Allan discussed in Chapter Two is heading for some theory building as other professors have picked up the idea. Peters' comments have re-inspired him to follow up on it. In the meantime, both of us have made mini-lectures a standard feature of our introductory classes.

On a statewide level with our action research network, we are now sorting out the themes and findings that keep emerging in the action research network projects through repeated use of the same interventions on the same problems across the state. We hope to be able to point to common patterns and a number of consistently successful interventions so others might try similar activities on a statewide or nationwide level.

We are also engaging in a research project (not action research this time) to evaluate the lasting effects of practitioner involvement in action research. We are investigating the lasting systemic effects of action research within employing institutions and lasting changes in both the practices and attitudes of practitioners. At this point, we know of at least three citywide education institutions that have radically changed their administrative procedures across an entire region based on the findings of their teacher-researcher staff members. We know of several action researchers who have said involvement in action research has changed their practice and their way of seeing; one has said it has "changed her professional life," and all have said they see professional development differently. But we mainly have learned that all of us "mere mortals" can learn from one another. We have learned that we can learn from our own practice in systematic ways. We have learned that we can support each other's efforts in ways that are tangible to the students we are committed to serve and appreciated by employers who have encouraged risk taking.

Peters has noted that he bases his comments on his own beliefs and experiences, affirming that we all begin with our own lives and the point where we are most comfortable. We wonder if a book can ever really capture the ever-changing growth that Peters asks for. Practitioners practice—they usually do not publish. Teaching knowledge is often passed on in the staff room and on the job. This is an area of changing, personalized, experience-based knowledge. We look at the fact that most of the knowledge in both the action research and the participatory research domains is oral; almost all of Myles Horton's "writing" was in the form of interviews (for example, Moyers, 1982). This is the exciting world of *action,* which printed words often fail to capture.

If this sourcebook falls short, as it may where personal growth is concerned, we can only say that were readers to join any of us in our training or research work, they would find out so much more about the personal growth and change each of us has experienced. Sadly, extensive orality also means the world of education can be a rather isolating one where practitioners live with degrees of the "quiet desperation" that Thoreau spoke of. We often keep our triumphs, our failures, and our insecurities mainly to ourselves. We do not share personal feelings and professional concerns with others on the job very much, let alone in teacher newsletters, monographs, or sourcebooks. We typically do not share until we find the right unthreatening circumstances and the right level of trust. Action research changes this.

Action research practitioners' planning meetings take place across tables covered with pizza, cookies, coffee, and notebooks. People are constantly jumping up to flipcharts, chalkboards, and overhead projectors. Everyone is intensely trying to figure out what each other's professional problem is. People are studying the proposed interventions, asking why someone's intervention is not working well enough. People are asking, "What should I do now?"—a phenomenon almost unheard of in an educational institution's staff room or a workshop with an expert at the front of the room. In an action research context, "Why are you doing this, not that?" is an exciting dynamic, not an accusation. If only the readers could join us in our classroom and tutoring settings to see learners debating issues, watching progress, investigating the unknown side by side with every adult in the room. Here is where teacher and student roles drop away. Here is *action* research where one gains professional and personal growth. It occurs to us that a sourcebook like this is perhaps the worst way to "discuss" the dynamics of action research. But it is a way to get others talking.

Peters is right in saying that action research is not a tight, linear process, even if we may have suggested this in giving guidelines as a means for practitioners to get started. Peters is right in saying that there is no one way to do action research. Peters is also right in saying that action research is not stagnant;

it is alive. It is a way to learn by doing and, as Lewin (1948) used to say, it is a way to do by learning. In all of these ways, we are in complete agreement.

In closing, we encourage every reader to give action research a try, since to try is surely "to envisage things as they could be otherwise . . . to make present what is absent, to summon up a condition that is not yet" (Greene, 1988, p. 16). To try is what matters.

References

Argyris, C. *Reasoning, Learning and Action: Individual and Organizational.* San Francisco: Jossey-Bass, 1982.

Blunt, A. "The Future of Adult Education Research." In R. Garrison (ed.), *Research Perspectives in Adult Education.* Malabar, Fla.: Krieger, 1994.

Bourdieu, P. "Systems of Education and Systems of Thought: New Directions for the Sociology of Education." In M.F.D. Young (ed.), *Knowledge and Control.* London: Collier-Macmillan, 1971.

Cervero, R. M. *Effective Continuing Education for Professionals.* San Francisco: Jossey-Bass, 1988.

Cotton, W. "The Challenge Confronting American Adult Education." *Adult Education,* 1964, 14 (2), 80–87.

Courtney, S. "Defining Adult and Continuing Education." In S. B. Merriam and P. M. Cunningham (eds.), *Handbook of Adult and Continuing Education.* San Francisco: Jossey-Bass, 1989.

Freire, P. *Pedagogy of the Oppressed.* New York: Seabury Press, 1973.

Greene, M. *The Dialectic of Freedom.* New York: Teachers College Press, 1988.

Guba, E. G., and Lincoln, Y. S. *Effective Evaluation: Improving the Usefulness of Evaluation Results Through Responsive and Naturalistic Approaches.* San Francisco: Jossey-Bass, 1981.

Kemmis, S., and McTaggart, R. (eds.). *The Action Research Planner.* Geelong, Australia: Deakin University Press, 1984.

Lewin, K. *Resolving Social Conflicts.* New York: HarperCollins, 1948.

Merriam, S. "How Research Produces Knowledge." In J. M. Peters, P. J. Jarvis, and Associates, *Adult Education: Evolution and Achievements in a Developing Field of Study.* San Francisco: Jossey-Bass, 1991.

Merriam, S., and Simpson, E. *A Guide to Research for Educators and Trainers of Adults.* Malabar, Fla.: Krieger, 1984.

Moyers, B. "The Adventures of a Radical Hillbilly: An Interview with Myles Horton." *Appalachian Journal,* 1982, 8 (4), 248–285.

Schön, D. *The Reflective Practitioner.* New York: Basic Books, 1983.

B. ALLAN QUIGLEY *is associate professor and regional director of adult education at Pennsylvania State University and director of the Pennsylvania Action Research Network.*

GARY W. KUHNE *is assistant professor of adult education at Pennsylvania State University and an evaluator/trainer in the Pennsylvania Action Research Network.*

INDEX

Accountability, 38

Action phase, 24, 25, 34, 39; in action research cycle, 27; in church participation case study, 48; in homeless shelter learner participation case study, 53; in hospital infection control case study, 60; implementation and observation (step 4) in, 28, 34; in interactive teleconferencing case study, 58; in museum education case study, 44–45; in prison tutor retention case study, 51; questions for, 39. *See also* Implementation and observation (step 4)

Action research: as challenge to traditional methodologies/ideologies, 1, 5–6, 12–14; controversy and, 73; in corporations, 4; critical perspective of, 1; definitions of, 14–15, 64–65; emancipatory, 15, 16, 17, 18, 74–75, 76–77, 78; ethics in, 80–85; extrapolation of, 1, 38–39, 41; formal versus informal settings and, 1; four steps of, 14–15, 16; in future of adult education research, 12–14; and gradual change in traditional adult education, 10–12; growing awareness of, in adult education, 5–6; institutional change focus in, 15, 17–18; international versus United States, 4, 9; iterative nature of, 26, 68, 71; in K–12 public education system, 1, 4, 9–10, 14, 15; labels used for, 14; participatory research versus, 16, 65–66, 76–79; practical, 15, 16, 17, 65, 66, 75, 76–77; step-by-step versus construct-as-you-go approach to, 68–70. *See also* Collaborative research; Interests/intentions; Participatory research; Research

Action research, adult education: aims of, 16, 65–66, 75–79; appropriate and inappropriate uses of, 26; case studies of, 41–61; centrist position in, 76–77; characteristics of, 14–15, 23–24; collective usefulness of, 36–38; core processes in, 24–26; critique of, 63–72; cycles of, 24, 26–27; emancipatory interests in, 17, 18, 74–75, 76–77, 78; ethics in, 80–85; examples of, 4, 36–38; extrap-

olation of, 1, 38–39, 41; framework for, 16–18; in future of adult education research, 12–14; growing awareness of, 5–6; ideologies of, 5, 6–9, 10–11, 13, 16, 75, 76–77; interests/intentions of, 16–18, 64–66, 79–82; lack of, 1, 4–5; limitations of, 26; motivation to implement, 27–28, 29, 79; oral versus written knowledge in, 84; possible practitioner questions for, 36–38; practical interests in, 17–18, 65, 66, 75, 76–77; in practice settings, case studies of, 41–61; in practice settings, model for, 23–40; problem posing in, 24, 25–26, 27, 77–79; questions for planning/implementing, 39–40, 68–69; six-step model of, 26–36, 39–40; six-step model of, in case studies, 41–61; six-step model of, critique of, 63–72; six-step model of, defense of, 73–85; step-by-step versus construct-as-you-go approach to, 68–70, 84; technical interests in, 17, 69, 74, 76; trial-and-error approach in, 23; use of, in practice settings, 23–40. *See also* Case studies; Cycles of action research; Interests/intentions

Action research planner, 39–40; critique of, 68–69

Action science, 17

Adams, F., 7, 18

Adult basic education (ABE), action research projects in, 36–37. *See also* Literacy

Adult education: accountability of, 38; change in, history of slow, 5, 75; collaborative research in, 9, 12–14; delivery structures of, 1, 6–7; excluded nontraditional forms of practice in, 7–8; formal, 1, 6, 7; future of research in, 12–14; history and structures of, 6–9; ideological divide in, 5, 6–9, 10–11, 13, 75, 76–77; informal, 1, 6–7; versus K–12 public education system, 1, 6; methodologies of, quantitative versus qualitative, 10–12; moral sensitivity in, 6; ownership of knowledge in, 5–6, 12–14;

ORDERING INFORMATION

NEW DIRECTIONS FOR ADULT AND CONTINUING EDUCATION is a series of paperback books that explores issues of common interest to instructors, administrators, counselors, and policy makers in a broad range of adult and continuing education settings—such as colleges and universities, extension programs, businesses, the military, prisons, libraries, and museums. Books in the series are published quarterly in Spring, Summer, Fall, and Winter and are available for purchase by subscription and individually.

SUBSCRIPTIONS cost $54.00 for individuals (a savings of 35 percent over single-copy prices) and $90.00 for institutions, agencies, and libraries. Standing orders are accepted. New York residents, add local sales tax for subscriptions. (For subscriptions outside the United States, add $7.00 for shipping via surface mail or $25.00 for air mail. Orders *must be prepaid* in U.S. dollars by check drawn on a U.S. bank or charged to VISA, MasterCard, or American Express.)

SINGLE COPIES cost $22.00 plus shipping (see below) when payment accompanies order. California, New Jersey, New York, and Washington, D.C., residents, please include appropriate sales tax. Canadian residents, add GST and any local taxes. Billed orders will be charged shipping and handling. No billed shipments to post office boxes. (Orders from outside the United States *must be prepaid* in U.S. dollars by check drawn on a U.S. bank or charged to VISA, MasterCard, or American Express.)

SHIPPING (SINGLE COPIES ONLY): $30.00 and under, add $5.50; to $50.00, add $6.50; to $75.00, add $7.50; to $100.00, add $9.00; to $150.00, add $10.00.

ALL PRICES are subject to change.

DISCOUNTS FOR QUANTITY ORDERS are available. Please write to the address below for information.

ALL ORDERS must include either the name of an individual or an official purchase order number. Please submit your order as follows:
    Subscriptions: specify series and year subscription is to begin
    Single copies: include individual title code (such as ACE 59)

MAIL ALL ORDERS TO:
    Jossey-Bass Publishers
    350 Sansome Street
    San Francisco, CA 94104-1342

PHONE subscriptions or single-copy orders toll-free at (888) 378-2537 or at (415) 433-1767 (toll call).

FAX orders toll-free to: (800) 605-2665.

FOR SUBSCRIPTION SALES OUTSIDE OF THE UNITED STATES, contact any international subscription agency or Jossey-Bass directly.